The Mermaid Mama:

NAVIGATING MOTHERHOOD AND THE TIDES OF LIFE

Lauren M. Debick

The Mermaid Mama:

NAVIGATING MOTHERHOOD AND THE TIDES OF LIFE

Lauren M. Debick

Ocala, Florida, U.S.A.

Cover design and page layout by: Nancy R. Koucky, nrkdesigns.com
Edited by: Karin Nicely Lord, serenpublishing.com

979-8-218-82681-9 (paperback)
979-8-234-00378-2 (e-book)
Printed in the United States of America

Published by
Camellia Creative Solutions, LLC
Ocala, Florida, U.S.A.

Camellia Creative Solutions

laurendebick.com

Dedication

To my wild, wonderful bunch of boys,
Andrew, Landyn, Layken, Ayden, Rylan, Juneau, and Gus:
Life with you is full, messy, magical, and mine.

To Andrew, my partner in every sense:
Thank you for your love, your patience, your steady presence,
and for holding it all down while I followed the call to write.

To my mom:
Thank you for your unwavering love, your courage, and your imagination:
You were the one who sang mermaid songs with me,
turned the back porch into an underwater world,
and taught me the magic of play and possibility.

To my friends, soul sisters, and the incredible village that surrounds me:
Thank you for showing up, cheering me on,
and walking beside me through every season.

And to Marley, who spent 17 years by my side:
Thank you for your quiet love. Though no longer earthside,
your paw prints remain with me always.

This book was written with all of you in mind
because none of it happens alone, and I'm so grateful it didn't have to.

Contents

Introduction:

Becoming the Mermaid Mama

I have wanted to write a book for as long as I can remember. Writing has always been my outlet, my way of making sense of the world. I vividly recall being around nine years old, sitting at my mom's electronic typewriter, the one she had bought to help with her nursing school assignments. That typewriter was a portal for me. I think it only displayed about four rows of text at a time, but that didn't matter. I would sit for hours, lost in my imagination, typing out stories, each one an adventure, each one a piece of me. Even as I grew older, the dream of publishing a book never faded; it simply waited in the background, patiently lingering, until I was ready to give it form.

The challenge was never a lack of ideas; if anything, I had too many. My mind brimmed with possibilities, but trying to condense them into one cohesive message felt impossible. Even more challenging was the battle to find my authentic voice. For a long time, I filtered my ideas through what I thought would be acceptable, mainstream, and "safe." I believed if I didn't reveal too much of my true self, I would be taken more seriously.

For years, I carefully curated the image of a capable business professional, a career woman who got things done, the one people could count on to make things happen. And yes, I am that person. I still am. But I am also a dreamer. A believer in magic. A friend to the trees. A lover of the ocean. Someone who stares at the clouds and lets the wind carry my thoughts. My head is often up in the sky, while my heart belongs to the sea.

For a long time, I didn't know how to reconcile these two sides of myself, the driven professional and the free-spirited wanderer. I worried that if people saw the whole of me, they might question my credibility. But becoming a stepmom and then twin mom has changed that perspective entirely.

I never thought I wanted children. I had extreme anxiety about pregnancy and had made peace with the idea that being a biological mother wasn't part of my journey. I also feared losing myself, of becoming known only as "so-and-so's mom," as if motherhood would erase all the other pieces of me. But the irony is, I was less myself before my twins arrived than I am now. They helped me rediscover who I truly am. They pulled the loose, scattered threads of my identity together and wove them into the tapestry of the woman I was meant to be.

At my core, I'm a communicator, a connector, and a soul driven by purpose. I believe in creating meaningful impact through strategy, community building, and a deep commitment to our planet. Whether it's podcasting, writing, or sparking intentional conversations, I strive to uplift others and inspire positive change.

My life has been a mosaic of passions, identities, and shifting tides. From the earliest days, I've always felt a pull toward the water and toward wonder. My mom and I would sing mermaid songs in the pool, our voices bubbling up with laughter. She would decorate the back porch with streamers in every shade of blue and green to make it look like we were under the ocean. I still remember the first time I slipped into a mermaid tail and swam. It was magical. In those moments, I felt completely free, fully myself, and deeply connected to something bigger. That spark of joy and freedom has stayed with me.

When I visited California at twelve years old, I knew I wanted to live somewhere with palm trees and sunshine. Years later, when I had the opportunity to take a job in Florida, I didn't hesitate. I spent every moment I could near the ocean.

Becoming the Mermaid Mama wasn't a sudden shift; it was a slow, soulful unfolding. It's the merging of my childhood enchantment with the realness of motherhood, career, and the currents of everyday life. It's about choosing presence over perfection, and wonder over weariness, again and again.

In 2018, years before this book came to life, I started a blog called *Mermaids & Mana.* It was a quiet reclamation of my voice. A creative outlet. A space where I could write freely about life, sustainability, spirituality, joy, and the healing power of nature.

At the time, I didn't know exactly what the blog was going to be, but I knew it was a call back to myself. I had been feeling unmoored, like I was losing touch with the version of me that once spent hours dreaming, writing, creating. *Mermaids & Mana* gave me a way to explore what mattered to me, including my connection to nature, my growing interest in eco-conscious living, my love for the symbolic, the magical, and the meaningful.

That blog was a breadcrumb on the path back to my full identity. And like so many things in life, it came full circle.

It was through that quiet unfolding of writing, reflecting, reconnecting that I began to remember who I was beyond the roles and routines. And in that remembering, the mermaid kept appearing as a guide and led me to reflect upon what mermaids actually mean to me and why they resonate with me so much.

Mermaids live at the edge of two worlds, gracefully straddling the mystical and the practical, the wild and the anchored. It didn't take long for me to see that I've been doing the same all along.

The mermaid represents harmony, adaptability, and strength, all qualities essential for motherhood and life. She exists between two worlds, navigating both with grace. She is untamed yet wise, fluid yet powerful. She is a bridge between the mystical and the real.

That duality is what speaks to me most. Mermaids live between land and sea, and I, too, live in between worlds as the ambitious career woman and the free spirit, the devoted mother and the independent creator. For years,

I fought to keep these aspects of myself separate, believing they couldn't coexist. But motherhood, especially twin motherhood, has taught me that harmony is not about choosing one identity over another; it's about learning to flow between them, just like the ocean.

The mermaid knows when to dive deep and when to surface.

She is wild and wise, intuitive and strong.

She doesn't choose between ambition and softness.

She holds both.

And that's what this book is about: learning to live as both.

Embracing the mermaid archetype offers me a powerful metaphor for navigating the complex currents of motherhood with grace, strength, and adaptability. Mermaids, who are often depicted as creatures of beauty and mystery, are also symbols of resilience and fluidity, perfectly poised to embody the modern mother's journey. Like a mermaid, mothers must learn to dive deep into the emotional depths of their families' needs while maintaining their own sense of self. By embodying the grace of a mermaid, a mother can handle life's challenges with confidence, even when the seas of life are turbulent.

The mermaid's strength lies not only in her ability to swim against strong tides but also in her connection to both the watery world below and the human world above. For mothers, this duality mirrors the harmony we must maintain between nurturing our children and pursuing our own dreams and goals. The adaptability of a mermaid reminds us to embrace change and flow with life's unpredictable waves, recognizing that resilience often comes from flexibility and creativity. Whether it's navigating the ever-changing demands of parenting or integrating career aspirations with family life, the mermaid archetype inspires a me to move fluidly through transitions.

Mermaids also symbolize a deep connection with nature and intuition. We, too, can benefit from this connection by trusting our instincts and grounding ourselves in our values. The mermaid archetype encourages us to honor our unique strengths, letting go of perfection and embracing authenticity. By seeing ourselves as graceful yet fierce, nurturing yet independent, we can thrive not by trying to conquer the ocean but by learning to swim with it, charting our own unique course. This perspective fosters not only self-compassion but also a sense of empowerment that ripples through every aspect of motherhood. And when considering our connection to nature, we're reminded of our responsibility to care for Mother Earth—living in harmony with the natural world and making choices that support a more sustainable, soul-aligned life.

Embracing the mermaid archetype is more than a metaphor; it's a call to step into your role as a mother with confidence, compassion, and a commitment to living authentically. Like the mermaid, you have the power to navigate the challenges of motherhood with grace, strength, and adaptability. As you dive into the depths of caregiving, career, and personal growth, remember that your unique blend of intuition and resilience is your greatest asset. Trust yourself to chart a path that honors both your family and your own well-being.

Now is the time to embrace your role with intention and purpose. Swim boldly into each new challenge, knowing that you are equipped with the grace to navigate it, the strength to overcome it, and the adaptability to thrive through it. Let the mermaid within remind you that you are both nurturing and powerful, deeply connected to the world around you and capable of shaping it for the better. Take a deep breath, trust your instincts, and move forward with confidence and compassion, leaving a legacy of love, wellness, and positive impact.

As I dive into the depths of my journey, I've come to understand that finding harmony in motherhood, career, wellness, and eco-conscious living is not unlike the movement of the tides, sometimes calm, sometimes wild, but always in motion. Being a twin mom, a stepmom, a career-driven woman, and an advocate for positive change, it often feels like I am navigating ever-changing waves.

This book, *The Mermaid Mama*, is a reflection of that journey. It is a story of embracing every facet of motherhood, career, and personal growth while honoring the rhythms of nature and the need for authenticity. Just as a mermaid is both ethereal and powerful, I believe we, too, can embody those same qualities as we nurture ourselves and others while remaining anchored in who we truly are.

The Mermaid Mama is my message of connection to the women who are navigating multiple roles as mothers, creators, leaders, caregivers, and dreamers.

It's a story of integration, of finding harmony between motherhood and personal growth, ambition and softness, nature and nurture.

It's a celebration of living with intention.

Of reconnecting to the Earth, your body, your breath.

Of finding joy in both the ocean and the shore.

My hope is to inspire other women to embrace their own journey, to find strength in the roles they play, and to live with purpose, grace, and a little bit of magic.

This book isn't just about inspiration, though; it's also about action.

In these pages, you will find journal prompts, reflective exercises, and activities to help you dive deeper into your own transformation. Whether you're a mom, an entrepreneur, a creative spirit, or someone simply looking for more harmony in your life, these guided reflections will help you reconnect with yourself, embrace your many roles, and find harmony in the ebb and flow of daily life.

So, whether you're in the depths of motherhood, drifting somewhere between your dreams and your duties, or standing at the edge of a new chapter, know this:

You are a force. A creator. A woman with depth and wisdom. A mermaid who is capable of existing in both worlds, embracing the ocean of motherhood while also walking boldly onto the shore of her own dreams.

You don't have to choose.

You can be both.

You already are.

So, to all the mothers, dreamers, and mermaids-at-heart, this is your invitation to embrace your inner spirit and to find joy in the ebb and flow of life. Because we are not meant to stay in one place. We are meant to swim, to explore, and to rise and fall with the waves.

Let's dive in.

Part 1:

Navigating the Depths—
The Inner Work of a Mermaid Mama

Chapter 1

Navigating the Tides of Family Life and the Shore of Personal Goals

Motherhood doesn't come with a map, especially when you're navigating an ocean as vast and unpredictable as this one. It's not just about keeping your head above water; it's about learning to ride the tides, to anchor in what matters, and to trust yourself to keep swimming when the waves crash hardest. Motherhood is the ocean that is beautiful, relentless, and expansive. And when you're charting a course that blends nurturing a family with nurturing your own dreams, the current can feel both exhilarating and overwhelming.

This chapter begins at a time when I felt both deeply fulfilled and completely overwhelmed; this was a time when the beauty and brutality of early motherhood collided, demanding more of me than I thought I had to give. It's where the myth and the mess started to meet.

Motherhood has tested me in ways I never expected. Bringing home one newborn is a massive adjustment. Bringing home two? That's a whole different level of chaos. The first few months felt like survival mode as I was functioning on minimal sleep, constantly feeding, changing, and soothing two babies around the clock. The exhaustion was unlike anything I had ever known. There were nights when I sat in the dark with a baby in my arms while his twin brother cried uncontrollably in his crib because I wasn't holding him. Talk about mom guilt. Tears would stream down my face, and I wondered how I was going to get through the next hour, let alone the next day.

The lack of sleep impacted everything. It made simple tasks feel insurmountable. There were days I forgot whether I had eaten, and moments when the idea of showering felt like an impossible luxury. And while I had so much love for my babies, I sometimes felt like I was losing myself in the process.

As the twins grew, there were new challenges to face, including teething, meltdowns, and playing referee between two growing boys. I've found myself rearranging my entire day to pick up the boys from daycare when fevers spiked, and there have been a handful of times where I was quietly crying in the laundry room between loads of clothes that needed to be washed and deadlines that needed to be met. And then there are the bigger challenges: navigating finances, trying to find a home that fits our growing family, and wondering if I'll ever feel fully like myself again. I know I am not alone in feeling this way. A 2022 survey by *Motherly* found that 64% of mothers felt they had lost a sense of identity after becoming parents.[1] This identity shift is often coupled with a sense of invisibility or guilt for wanting personal space to dream, work, or even rest.

It's in these quiet moments, between loads of laundry and the weight of unspoken worries, that the ache for something more begins to rise. We start to crave clarity, not just sleep. We long to remember the parts of ourselves that existed before motherhood, and to imagine what might still be possible beyond it.

Other days, we long to pull ourselves onto the shore, to breathe, to dream, to remind ourselves we are not just caretakers; we are whole, multidimensional women with our own stories to write.

But let's be real—the ocean often demands more.

The tides of motherhood are ever shifting, with no clear instructions to guide each ebb and flow. While I was training for my first New York half marathon, I adhered to a dedicated 5 a.m. running schedule every Tuesday, Thursday, and Saturday like clockwork. But one week, everything changed.

1 Motherly. (2021). 2021 *State of Motherhood Survey Results*. Retrieved from https://www.mother.ly/news/2021-state-of-motherhood-survey

A nasty bug swept through our home, knocking both me and the twins off our feet. That week, my early morning miles were replaced with sleepless nights, rocking babies, offering comfort, and whispering lullabies instead of lacing up my shoes.

That week reminded me of something essential: motherhood doesn't pause for training schedules or personal goals. It flows according to its own rhythm, often pulling us in directions we didn't expect. And just when you think you've found your stride, the current changes.

The waves of responsibilities like feeding, nurturing, managing schedules, wiping noses, remembering doctor appointments, and offering emotional support can feel relentless. Some days, you're treading water, just trying to stay afloat. Other days, the ocean feels serene, filled with love, laughter, and those moments where time seems to slow down, reminding you why this journey is so beautiful.

The ocean isn't just about the sheer volume of tasks; it's about the deep emotional connection to our children, the way our hearts stretch and expand in ways we never imagined. It's about the overwhelming love, the fierce protectiveness, the way we instinctively know when something isn't right, and how we'd move mountains or swim across entire oceans to make things better for our little ones. But this deep, boundless love can also feel all-consuming, pulling us under if we're not careful.

And that's where the shore comes in.

The shore represents our personal growth, our ambitions, our need to be more than just a mother. I always dreamed of writing a book, but it wasn't until after becoming a mother that I felt the fierce drive to make it happen. Between early morning and late-night writing sessions, and any time I could grab in between, I was able to publish this book, slowly but surely stepping onto that shore. That makes every page written amid bottles, biting toddlers, and laundry piles a radical act of reclamation.

The shore is a reminder that we are not just here to serve but that we are here to live, to evolve, to create. The shore is the version of us that existed before motherhood and the version that will continue to grow alongside it.

But here's where the struggle lies: how do we exist in both places?

How do we honor the ocean, the relentless but beautiful pull of motherhood, while still reaching for the shore? How do we allow ourselves to step onto land, even for a moment, without feeling guilty for leaving the waves behind?

This is where the mermaid's wisdom comes in.

Mermaids don't just survive between two worlds; they *thrive* in both. They move fluidly between the depths and the surface, never truly leaving one behind for the other. And that's the mindset we, as mothers, need to embrace. It's not about finding balance, because let's be honest—balance doesn't exist. Sometimes, the waves will crash harder, and we'll have no choice but to stay in the ocean, giving our all to our children and our families. Other times, we'll find our way to the shore, reclaiming parts of ourselves that have been waiting to be seen again.

The key is in the ebb and flow.

It's understanding that motherhood and personal growth are not opposing forces; they are interconnected. It's allowing ourselves the grace to fully show up for our families without losing sight of our own needs and dreams. It's knowing that taking time for ourselves is not selfish; it's essential. A mother who nurtures her own passions, creativity, and well-being is not abandoning her family; she's showing them what it looks like to live fully. She's leading by example, teaching her children that they, too, should honor their dreams.

So, how do we do this? How do we become mermaids in our own lives?

Just like the tides, we rise and recede between deep devotion to our families and the quiet pull of our own desires. And while learning to live between these two realms is its own kind of magic, it's only the beginning. The real journey begins when we pause long enough to ask ourselves: *What truly matters to me? What are the values that guide my choices, the dreams I refuse to bury, and the priorities I want to honor as both a mother and a woman?*

Before we can chart a course that feels aligned, we need to find our inner compass.

In the next chapter, we'll begin that process by identifying the values that shape your choices, and from there, we'll create your compass and a personal mantra that can guide you through even the most turbulent days. It will be a phrase you can return to, your own steady rhythm when the world feels like too much.

Reflection Prompt:

As we prepare to explore to create your compass and mantra, I invite you take a few moments to journal on the following:

- *What do I want to feel more of in my life right now?*
- *What keeps me grounded when life feels chaotic?*
- *What do I need to hear on the days when I forget my own strength?*

Let these questions open the door to deeper awareness. The clarity you uncover will become the foundation for the compass and mantra we'll shape together next.

Chapter 2

Finding Your Compass: Identifying Your Priorities and Navigating Forward

If chapter 1 was about acknowledging the waves, the challenges, beauty, and duality of motherhood, then this chapter is about tuning into the internal compass that helps you move through them with clarity and intention.

In motherhood, we exist between two worlds, the ever-moving ocean of family life and the grounding shore of personal aspirations. Some days, we're fully submerged in the depths of caregiving, completely immersed in meeting the needs of our children and loved ones. Other days, we catch a glimpse of the shore, which includes our personal goals, passions, and dreams calling out to us, waiting to be honored.

In the chaos of caregiving, career-building, and day-to-day survival, it's easy to lose sight of what truly matters to *you*. Not the expectations placed on you, not the comparison game, not the mental checklist running in the background but the values that light you up and help you feel aligned.

These values are your anchors.

And from them, you'll create a compass and mantra, simple but powerful tools that bring you back to center when the waves feel overwhelming.

Just as sailors rely on a compass to navigate uncharted waters, we, too, need a guide, something that keeps us aligned with what truly matters, no matter how strong the waves become. In this chapter, we'll walk through a series of exercises designed to help you define your inner compass, the combination of values, priorities, and personal truths that guide your decisions and keep you rooted in who you are. This will be the foundation you return to when life feels noisy or unclear.

Your compass is made up of 3 key elements:

- Your priorities: *The things that matter most to you in this season of life.*
- Your values: *The guiding principles that shape how you live, work, and love.*
- Your energy: *Where you invest your time and attention, ensuring your daily actions align with your bigger vision.*

And there's one more piece, a thread that ties it all together. Your personal mantra.

A mantra is a phrase, affirmation, or sentence that brings you back to your center. It's a calming whisper when the chaos gets loud. It's a quiet declaration of who you are and what matters.

For me, it's: *"When you feel good, you do good."*

This reminds me that I'm at my best when I'm nourished, supported, and grounded. It's not about being perfect; it's about being aligned. It's foundational. When I take care of myself, body, mind, and spirit, I show up as a more grounded, present, and intentional mother, partner, and woman who can create ripples of positive impact around me.

Without a clear compass, it's easy to drift aimlessly, caught in the undercurrent of obligations, guilt, and overwhelm. This sentiment is echoed by a recent survey where 79% of mothers reported feeling invisible after having children,[2] highlighting the necessity of defining what is most important to you. When you establish your priorities, decision-making becomes easier, and the balance between motherhood and personal growth feels more intentional.

---

2 Kappes, W. (2023, October 27). *79 Percent of Moms Feel Invisible, New Survey Shows.* The Bump. Retrieved from https://www.thebump.com/news/state-of-invisibility

The Moment I Realized My Priorities Were My True Compass

I have not always been the best at setting priorities. For a long time, I let life push me around like driftwood being tumbled against the rocks, unsure of where I stood or what I really wanted.

One of the biggest wake-up calls for me was when I made the decision to quit smoking. At the time, I was deeply addicted, though I had never called it that before now. I convinced myself it was just a habit, something I could quit anytime I wanted. But deep down, I knew it had a hold on me.

Then, I met Andrew (my now husband). I knew I wanted a future with him, and I knew I wanted to be healthier, not just for him but for me. That desire, that priority, outweighed my addiction. And for the first time, I had something stronger than my excuses: a clear, defined reason to change.

The same thing happened when my twins were born. I had spent years grinding in my career, pushing myself to excel, believing I had to show up in a certain way to be successful. But when my boys arrived, my definition of success changed. I realized I didn't want to give 100% to work while giving what was left of me to my family. I still wanted to work. I still wanted to make an impact. But I knew I needed to find an environment that supported the harmony I craved. So, I adjusted my sails, and I made a career shift that allowed me to still do fulfilling work while prioritizing my family. That decision wasn't easy, but it was clear because I had already defined what mattered most.

When I found myself juggling the demands of motherhood, career, and my personal goals, I often felt like I was swimming against the current. There were sleepless nights, moments of self-doubt, and the ever-present question: "Am I enough?" But every time I returned to my compass, I found clarity. I was reminded that it's okay to pause, to recalibrate, and to adjust my course to re-align with my priorities.

Identifying your priorities isn't about doing everything at once or being perfect in every area of your life. It's about being intentional. This is especially pertinent considering that 71% of mothers report being most strongly defined by their motherhood, with the number rising to 78% among younger moms.[3] By clarifying what brings you joy and fulfillment beyond motherhood, you can create a more harmonious and intentional life.

And as you reflect on your priorities, you might begin to notice a few themes in the shape of words or ideas that come up again and again. Maybe it's *freedom*, or *peace*, or *impact*. These threads aren't just clues to what matters most; they're the building blocks of your mantra. Let them guide you.

To start, ask yourself:

- What brings me joy? What activities, moments, or experiences genuinely light me up?
- What makes me feel fulfilled? What aspects of my life leave me with a deep sense of purpose?
- What are my non-negotiables? What boundaries am I unwilling to compromise?
- What does success look like for me? Not what success means to the world but what it means to me.

Once you've identified these priorities, take a hard look at how you're currently spending your time. Does your daily schedule reflect what truly matters to you? If not, it's time to realign.

Understanding Your Compass

Every mermaid has her compass, a tool not just for direction but for purpose, growth, and grace. As mothers, career professionals, and individuals navigating a sea of responsibilities, we, too, must find our compass, a guiding force that helps us make sense of challenges and steer toward the life we envision.

---

3 DFWChild. (2023). Identity Crisis: *Rediscovering Yourself in Motherhood.* Retrieved from https://dfwchild.com/identity-crisis-rediscovering-yourself-in-motherhood

The Mermaid Mama's Compass isn't a physical object, though you can create a visual representation of it as a reminder. It's a blend of values, priorities, and the tools we rely on to keep our course steady.

For me, my compass is anchored by 3 key elements:

1. Wellness as a Foundation

A healthy mind and body create the energy we need to face challenges. This doesn't mean perfection; it means harmony. It's about listening to your body when it whispers so it doesn't have to scream.

For me, wellness means:

- Running, paddleboarding, and being near the water. These activities ground me and restore my energy.
- Prioritizing mental and emotional well-being. Therapy, journaling, and personal growth work are non-negotiables.
- Understanding that self-care is not selfish. If I don't take care of myself, I can't fully show up for the people I love.

2. Clear Communication as a Tool

Just like the ocean's tides, life is in constant motion. Communicating our needs, setting boundaries, and expressing our dreams clearly are vital in keeping our direction intact. As women, it's easy to fall into the trap of putting others' needs above our own. But remember, a compass only works when it's true to its center.

3. Creating a Positive Impact as the Map

My mission is to make an impact—in my home, my community, and beyond.

- I give back through plogging (picking up trash while jogging), supporting causes I care about, and being active in my community.

- I use my voice through coaching, speaking, and podcasting to empower others.
- I teach my children resilience, kindness, and a sense of responsibility toward the planet.

Just like the tides, our influence ripples outward. What we do within our own waters extends into something greater.

The beauty of being a Mermaid Mama is that we don't just survive the challenges; we grow because of them. We learn to trust our intuition, to embrace our imperfections, and to honor our unique journey.

Your compass is yours to design. Fill it with the values that matter most to you, and use it to guide you through every wave, every tide, and every storm.

Let it remind you that no matter how vast the ocean, you are never truly lost. You have the strength to navigate with purpose, the grace to adapt to change, and the wisdom to know that every challenge is an opportunity to grow.

Now, it's time to gather all of these insights, the values that light you up, the wellness practices that sustain you, the priorities that define this chapter of your life, and craft something lasting: your Mermaid Mama Compass.

Along the way, you'll also create your personal mantra, a phrase that will become your anchor when life feels unsteady and your North Star when you need direction.

Let's Build Your Compass

In the next section, we'll work through exercises to define your core values, clarify your priorities, and create a personal compass that will help you navigate both the ocean and the shore with confidence.

So, Mermaid Mama, take a deep breath. Hold your compass close. And remember, the sea is vast, but so is your strength.

Exercise 1: Identifying Core Values

Objective: Define the values that serve as your internal compass, guiding you through life's waves with clarity and purpose.

Journal Prompts:

- *What are the top 5 values that guide my life?*
- *Why do these matter to me?*

Step 1: Brainstorm Values

Write down a list of words that resonate with you, such as:

- Love
- Adventure
- Balance
- Authenticity
- Success
- Service
- Freedom
- Wellness

Step 2: Narrow It Down

Circle 5 values that feel most aligned with who you are and who you want to be.

Step 3: Reflection

For each of your 5 values, answer:

- How does this value show up in my daily life?
- Where am I honoring this value, and where am I neglecting it?

- How can I align my choices with this value more intentionally?

Exercise 2: Calibrating Your Compass—Wellness Check-In

Objective: Assess how well you are taking care of yourself physically, mentally, emotionally, financially, and spiritually.

Journal Prompts:

- *When do I feel my best physically, mentally, emotionally, financially, and spiritually?*
- *What habits or routines support that feeling?*
- *Where do I feel the most out of balance, and why?*

Step 1: Draw a Wellness Pie Chart

Create a circle divided into 5 sections:

- Physical Wellness (Movement, nutrition, sleep)
- Mental Wellness (Mindset, learning, creativity)
- Emotional Wellness (Self-care, relationships, boundaries)
- Financial Wellness (Budgeting, saving, financial confidence, spending habits)
- Spiritual Wellness (Connection, purpose, mindfulness)

Step 2: Self-Assessment

Shade in each section based on how fulfilled you currently feel (0–100%). The darker the shading, the more fulfilled you feel about that aspect.

Step 3: Action Plan

For each category, write one small change you can make this week to improve how you feel in that area.

Example:

- *Physical:* Take a morning walk 3 times this week.
- *Mental:* Read 10 pages of a book that inspires me.
- *Emotional:* Set a boundary with my time and energy.
- *Financial:* Review my monthly spending and set one small savings goal.
- *Spiritual:* Spend 5 minutes in stillness each morning.

Exercise 3: Your Compass Affirmation—A Guiding Mantra

Objective: Craft a personal mantra that reflects your values, priorities, and journey.

Journal Prompts:

- *If my life had a guiding mantra, what would it be?*
- *What words empower me when I feel lost?*

Step 1: Write Down Words That Inspire You

Example: Strength, grace, purpose, flow, harmony, resilience, love

Step 2: Create Your Mantra

Examples:

"I navigate life's waves with grace, strength, and purpose."

"I am both the ocean and the shore, embracing the ebb and flow of life."

Step 3: Make It Part of Your Daily Life

- Write your mantra somewhere visible.
- Repeat it in moments of doubt.
- Use it as an anchor when making decisions.

After completing these exercises, summarize your core compass elements:

My Top 3 Core Values:

1.

2.

3.

My Priorities in This Season of Life:

Family:

Career:

Wellness:

One Change I Will Make This Week to Align with My Compass:

My Personal Compass Mantra:

You've just built something beautiful, a compass that's rooted in who you are and who you're growing into. Your values, your priorities, and your personal mantra are more than words on a page; they are tools to return to, again and again.

Let your mantra carry you. Let it be a mirror and a map. And remember, Mermaid Mama, this journey isn't about perfection. It's about presence. You're doing beautifully.

You have the strength to navigate with purpose, the grace to adapt to change, and the wisdom to know that every challenge is an opportunity to grow.

But having your compass is only the beginning. Now comes the real question:

How do you use it when the waters get choppy?

Welcome to the next phase of this journey, where we learn to ride the waves.

Chapter 3

Riding the Waves: Embracing Flexibility and Flow in Motherhood

Even with your Mermaid Mama Compass in hand, your values clearly defined, and your direction steady, there may be moments when you still question yourself. That voice might whisper:

- "Who do you think you are to lead like this?"
- "You're not *really* qualified."
- "You're just faking it better than most."

That's not your truth speaking. That's imposter syndrome.

Imposter syndrome affects so many women, particularly those juggling multiple roles like motherhood, career, and leadership. It's the internal narrative that tells us we're not good enough, even when all evidence points to the contrary.

In fact, research shows that up to 70% of people will experience imposter syndrome at some point in their lives.[4] For working moms and high-achieving women, these feelings often intensify in moments of transition, like returning to work after maternity leave, launching a new creative project, or trying something outside your comfort zone.

---

4 Bravata, D. M., Watts, S. A., Keefer, A. L., Madhusudhan, D. K., Taylor, K. T., Clark, D. M., Nelson, R. S., Cokley, K. O., & Hagg, H. K. (2020). Prevalence, predictors, and treatment of impostor syndrome: A systematic review. ***Journal of General Internal Medicine, 35***(4), 1252–1275. https://doi.org/10.1007/s11606-019-05364-1

I recently had a powerful conversation on my podcast with my friend and guest, R.J., an expert in helping people navigate these types of situations. In this empowering episode, we explored how imposter syndrome isn't really a syndrome at all, meaning there is nothing that needs to be fixed. Instead, it is a feeling that comes from our inner voice that questions whether we belong in the very spaces we've worked hard to reach.

R.J. offered a fresh and compassionate perspective on these feelings, sharing how imposter feelings aren't a sign of inadequacy but instead are often a signal that we're standing at the edge of growth. He talked about how we can begin to transform self-doubt into confidence, shift our mindset to embrace aspiration, and practice grace and self-acceptance along the way.

As he said so memorably:

"I have never, not one time, worked with someone who has been experiencing imposter feelings who wasn't always already engaged in a moment of aspiration."

That line stopped me in my tracks.

Because the truth is, having a strong sense of purpose doesn't mean you won't experience doubt. It means you care. And those moments of uncertainty? They don't make you an imposter. They make you human. Learning to move with them, not against them, is part of riding the waves.

I encourage you to listen to the full episode: "Reframing Imposter Syndrome: From Self-Doubt to Aspiring Forward." It's a powerful reminder that you are not alone, and that with compassion, curiosity, and courage, you can rewrite the stories you tell yourself.

But listening is just the beginning.

Because while awareness is a crucial first step, it's what we do with that awareness that truly shifts our experience. So, let's take it one step further. I want to offer you a few simple practices to help you move through those moments when doubt creeps in.

These aren't about fixing yourself because you were never broken to begin with. They're about anchoring in truth when the waves of insecurity try to pull you under.

Try This:

- Write down one role or title (e.g., mother, leader, creator) that feels a little intimidating to fully claim.
- Next to it, jot down proof that you're already showing up in that role (e.g., small wins, compliments received, things you've learned).
- Then rewrite the label: "I am learning to embody the role of ___ with authenticity and grace."

Let this next affirmation be your breath of calm in the swirl of doubt:

I am not an imposter; I am a woman in motion, growing into every role with grace, courage, and authenticity. My worth is not measured by perfection but by presence.

So, Mermaid Mama, when the tides of doubt rise, return to your compass. Re-center yourself in what you know to be true, not just in your head but in your heart.

Because navigating motherhood and life isn't about always feeling confident. It's about showing up with intention, even when the path feels uncertain.

And this brings us back to our next wave: embracing flexibility and flow. The truth is, motherhood is anything but predictable. One day, you're feeling like a powerhouse, crushing deadlines, remembering snack day, and even squeezing in a four-mile run. The next, you're scrambling to find matching socks, reheating your coffee for the fourth time, and silently thanking Ms. Rachel for holding your child's attention long enough for you to breathe. That's the rhythm of it all, the push and pull, the tides that change without warning.

In these moments, your compass matters most. Not because it gives you exact directions but because it reminds you who you are as the waves roll in. It's about giving yourself grace on the days that feel messy, being open to Plan B (or C or D), and recognizing that flexibility is one of your greatest strengths.

Self-care, too, becomes less about bubble baths and more about survival rituals: a morning walk to clear your mind, calling a friend instead of doom-scrolling, or taking five minutes to just sit in silence (yes, even if that silence is in a locked bathroom). I'll share some of the small practices that have helped me stay afloat when the waves got rough.

Because, Mermaid Mama, riding the waves isn't about always staying on top. It's about learning to move with the current, to find rhythm in the chaos, and to trust that even when you're off balance, you're still moving forward.

I love surfing. I'm not great at it, I don't go nearly as often as I'd like, and I wipe out more times than I care to count, but I love it anyway. The feeling of paddling out, catching even the smallest wave, and floating between sets is pure magic. Surfing has taught me more about motherhood than any parenting book ever could.

Sometimes you catch a wave and feel like you're flying. Other times, you get knocked under so hard it takes a second to remember which way is up. But the magic lies in showing up anyway, in trusting that the ocean will always offer another wave, in surrendering to the flow rather than resisting it.

Motherhood works the same way.

The truth is, motherhood (hell, life in general) isn't something you can plan down to the minute and expect it to always go as scheduled. You might have a beautifully color-coded planner or a carefully structured routine, but then your toddler gets sick, a deadline at work shifts, or you realize you've been so busy meeting everyone else's needs that you forgot to eat lunch.

We're often told to strive for balance, as if we could give equal attention to work, home, kids, wellness, friendships, and dreams in perfect portions every day. But balance, in that sense, is a myth.

I prefer the word *harmony*. Harmony acknowledges that life is a symphony of shifting priorities. Some days, your career takes center stage. Other days, it's the needs of your children or your own health. Harmony is not about doing everything at once; it's about being in tune with what or who needs you most in each moment. This perspective allows for the natural ebb and flow of priorities, acknowledging that some days, family may take precedence, while on others, personal aspirations come to the forefront.

It is a deep knowing of when to lean in and when to let go. It's about learning to ride the waves rather than trying to control the tide.

This shift in mindset is backed by data: a Pew Research Center study found that 45% of working mothers say balancing work and family responsibilities makes it harder to be a good parent.[5] Harmony offers an alternative that prioritizes flow over perfection. By seeking harmony, mothers can alleviate the pressure of meeting rigid standards and instead focus on creating a fulfilling and flexible life that honors both their family and personal ambitions.

Juggling family life and personal goals can often feel like a tug-of-war for many moms, even if you are trying to embrace flexibility and flow. But with a few intentional strategies, it's possible to create a sense of harmony, where both family responsibilities and personal aspirations are honored without one being sacrificed for the other. Think of it not as a perfect balance but as a fluid rhythm that shifts with your season of life. Here are some strategies to help you cultivate that harmony and move through motherhood with more flow and grace:

1. Involve the Family in Your Goals: Sometimes, the line between family and personal aspirations can be blurred in a way that feels fulfilling. For example, consider involving

---

5 Pew Research Center. (2013, December 11). ***Chapter 5: Balancing work and family***. In ***Modern Parenthood***. Retrieved from https://www.pewresearch.org/social-trends/2013/12/11/chapter-5-balancing-work-and-family/

your children in your personal pursuits, like exercising together or sharing a hobby. This not only allows you to nurture your personal growth but can also strengthen family bonds. I've started bringing my boys along on walks or stretching while they play. Movement helps me reset, and involving them reminds me that caring for myself doesn't have to mean separating from them; it can mean sharing that space.

2. Use Small Windows of Time: Progress on personal goals doesn't always need to happen in large blocks of time. Even in the busiest days, there are often small windows of opportunity, like during a child's nap, after they go to bed, or while waiting for a meeting. As moms, we can take advantage of these moments to chip away at goals, whether it's reading a few pages of a book, brainstorming for a project, or writing down thoughts for a journal. I personally write down thoughts and ideas on the notes app on my phone when ideas come to me throughout the day, and sometimes I brainstorm podcast topics during a stroller walk. Those little windows add up.

3. Practice Self-Care and Avoid Overcommitting: Our well-being is essential for giving to both our families and our personal goals. Making self-care a priority ensures we have the energy and mindset to handle both roles. Additionally, we can avoid the pressure of overcommitting by saying no to certain obligations and learning to be realistic about what can fit into our schedules (more on this soon). I used to think self-care meant spa days and silence. Now, self-care looks like taking a walk around the block or reading a few pages of a "romantasy" novel after the boys have gone to sleep. Self-care can be simple and still impactful.

4. Break Down Big Goals into Smaller Steps: Personal goals often feel overwhelming when approached as a whole.

Instead, break them down into smaller, more manageable tasks. This way, progress can be made little by little, and the sense of accomplishment from each small step builds momentum, making it easier to stay motivated. Writing this book didn't happen in long, uninterrupted writing sessions. It happened during naps, early mornings, long nights, and in the form of messy outlines between laundry cycles.

5. Incorporate Flexibility: Life with kids is unpredictable, and schedules can change in an instant. Taking a flexible approach allows us to adapt when plans don't go as expected. If a planned hour of personal time is disrupted, try to find another opportunity later in the day or week, so you can keep your goals on track without the stress of rigid expectations. My calendar now has wiggle room. I no longer feel guilty about shifting plans. Flexibility isn't failure; it's how we stay afloat.

6. Celebrate the Wins: It's important to acknowledge the accomplishments, big or small. Whether it's completing a personal project, getting a new opportunity, or simply managing to find time for yourself amidst the chaos, celebrating these moments can help you stay motivated and feel validated in both your family role and personal journey. I've learned to celebrate in ways that are important to me, like spending time outside, having dinner with a friend, saying yes to a beach day. It all matters.

By integrating these strategies into daily life, we are in a better position to create harmony between our family and personal goals. This is about setting us up for success in a place where both areas of life can thrive. It's about being intentional, setting realistic expectations, and carving out space for personal growth while being present for our families.

But harmony isn't just about calendars and checklists; it's also deeply personal. It's shaped by the examples we've seen, the habits we've inherited, and the moments that have left lasting imprints on our hearts. For me, that lesson came from watching someone I love give endlessly without ever refilling her own cup.

Watching my mom put everyone ahead of herself taught me something important: self-sacrifice without limits can take a toll. She's one of the most selfless people I know, but over the years, I saw how constantly putting her own needs last led to exhaustion, stress, and burnout. And that's when it clicked for me: if we don't make space to care for ourselves, eventually something gives.

And the beautiful thing? My mom is starting to see it, too. She's beginning to understand that caring for yourself isn't selfish; it's essential. She's finding new ways to rest, to say no, and to listen to her own needs after decades of putting everyone else first. Watching her begin that journey has reminded me that it's never too late to choose wellness.

Self-care isn't selfish; it's the very thing that allows us to care for others.

According to the American Psychological Association, nearly 70% of mothers say they feel overwhelmed by the pressure of balancing responsibilities.[6] If we don't create space to breathe, we'll drown in expectation.

So, I started running again. I prioritized walks outside, podcasting, writing, being near water. These are the things that help me feel like *me*. I'm not perfect at it, but I try. And when I feel good, everything else runs more smoothly too.

Motherhood doesn't follow a script. It's full of changing tides, unpredictable currents, and moments that catch us off guard. While we often focus on being flexible, adjusting our plans, and staying afloat amidst the chaos, there are other quiet but powerful forces that help us ride the waves: grace and gratitude.

Grace is the gentle current beneath the surface. It's the space we create to be imperfect, the kindness we extend when expectations aren't met, and

---

6 American Psychological Association. (2023). *Stress in America™ 2023: A nation grappling with collective trauma.* https://www.apa.org/news/press/releases/stress

the deep breath we take when everything feels like too much.

We're usually quick to offer grace to others, like a child melting down at bedtime, a friend who cancels last minute, a partner who forgets an errand. But when it comes to ourselves, we're often far less forgiving. We hold ourselves to impossible standards, forgetting that growth, like the tide, comes and goes in waves.

The truth is, flexibility without grace can feel like pressure, a demand to handle every change effortlessly. But when we allow grace to flow alongside our flexibility, we create a nurturing environment for ourselves to stumble, realign, and continue forward with softness and strength.

Embracing grace means:

- Allowing for the undone laundry, the skipped workout, or the drive-thru dinner (without guilt).
- Honoring our limitations as seasons, not failures.
- Remembering that showing up doesn't always mean showing up perfectly.

The other force that helps me ride the waves is gratitude.

Gratitude anchors me in the present. It reminds me that even on the hardest days, there's something good. A baby's giggle. The kindness of a stranger. That first sip of coffee. Research shows that people who regularly practice gratitude sleep better, feel more optimistic, and report greater emotional well-being.[7]

Here's what this looks like for me:

- I keep a small journal by my bed to jot down 10 things I'm grateful for each night.
- I send random texts to friends to say thank you for their support.

---

7 Emmons, R. A., & McCullough, M. E. (2003). Counting blessings versus burdens: An experimental investigation of gratitude and subjective well-being in daily life. *Journal of Personality and Social Psychology, 84(2)*, 377–389. https://doi.org/10.1037/0022-3514.84.2.377

- I have automatic reminders set up on my phone throughout the day inviting me to pause and think about something I am grateful for.

Gratitude doesn't erase the hard, but it softens it. It makes the ride feel less bumpy.

Like the ocean, we are powerful and ever-changing. When we meet ourselves with grace and gratitude, we not only weather the waves; we learn to dance with them.

As mothers and professionals, we often find ourselves pulled in a thousand directions, juggling the demands of work, family, and personal commitments. In the midst of this whirlwind, it's easy to forget to care for ourselves. But just as the ocean has its many ebbs and flows, so do our lives.

Embracing wellness is about finding harmony between the calm and the chaos, ensuring that we don't lose ourselves in the undertow. It's about showing up for others while also honoring our own needs, recognizing that our well-being is essential to everything we do.

Wellness isn't just about physical health; it's a holistic approach that encompasses mental, emotional, and spiritual well-being. In a world that moves at breakneck speed, we must make time to nurture ourselves. Whether it's carving out moments for quiet reflection, indulging in a hobby, or simply resting, these practices are more than luxuries—they are vital acts of self-preservation. It's often in the smallest moments of peace that we find the clarity and strength to keep going, just as the ocean's waves can calm and restore after the most turbulent storms.

When we allow ourselves to embrace wellness, we send a powerful message to ourselves and those around us. By prioritizing our well-being, we model self-care for our children, our colleagues, and our friends. We show that it's possible to care for others while still honoring our own needs.

Self-care doesn't have to be elaborate or time-consuming. In fact, the most sustainable rituals are the small, consistent choices we make to honor ourselves daily. When we're in the thick of motherhood, managing routines, supporting our families, and pursuing personal goals, it can be easy to forget that we are allowed to care for ourselves too.

But here's the truth, Mermaid Mama: Your well-being *is* the foundation. When you feel grounded, nourished, and seen, even by yourself, everything else flows more freely.

Here are some simple, soul-nurturing self-care practices that can help restore your energy and keep you connected to yourself, even during the busiest seasons.

Morning Grounding

- Gratitude Journal: Start your day by writing down 3 things you're grateful for. It's a small act that shifts your mindset and sets a positive tone.
- Hydration Routine: Drink a glass of water with lemon in the morning for a quick detox and hydration boost. A moment of care before the demands of the day begin.

Daily Micro-Moments

- Stretch or Walk: Even a 5- to 10-minute stretch or walk during nap time or after lunch can give your body and brain a reset.
- Affirmations: Place sticky notes with encouraging words in your bathroom or workspace. Little reminders like "You are doing enough" go a long way.
- Music Break: Play music that lifts your spirits—while prepping meals or tidying up, turn it into a mini joy ritual.

Nurturing Your Body

- Skincare Mini-Ritual: Invest in a simple routine with a cleanser, moisturizer, and SPF. It's quick, indulgent, and a way to reconnect with your reflection.
- Healthy Snacks: Keep nourishing options like almonds, fruit, or yogurt on hand. Fueling your body is an act of love.
- Short Exercise Videos: 10- to15-minute yoga or dance videos online can shift your whole mood (and it's okay if a toddler or two join in).

Evening Wind-Down

- Tea Time: Sip herbal tea while journaling or reading a few pages of a book. It signals to your body that it's time to rest.
- Tech-Free Hour: Power down screens an hour before bed to help improve sleep quality.
- Gratitude Reflection: Before sleep, list what went well, even the tiniest wins. This practice rewires your brain for joy.

Weekly Recharge

- Solo Outing: Grab coffee, visit a bookstore, or sit alone at the beach. Even just one hour of solitude can be deeply refreshing.
- Digital Detox Day: Take a break from social media to reclaim your focus and protect your energy.
- Creative Hobby: Paint, write, knit, sing—anything that lets you create without pressure or performance.

My Real-Life Recharge List

Here's what helps me stay well in the waves:

- Running outside and breathing in fresh air.
- Podcasting and writing as outlets for creativity and connection.
- Spending time in or near water as it centers me.
- Prioritizing rest, counseling, and moments of quiet reflection.
- Laughing with friends. Sharing meals. Fighting the urge to do it all alone.
- Saying no when it's not a good fit.
- Reading for joy. Working with purpose. Supporting causes I care about.
- Ordering dinner instead of cooking when that's what I need.
- Being flexible. Giving back. Asking for help.
- Creating space for who I am growing into.

These aren't checkboxes; they're lifelines. Choose the ones that resonate. Let go of the rest. Because taking care of yourself isn't about doing more; it's about choosing what matters most.

And what matters most can shift with the season you're in. Just like the ocean, motherhood moves in rhythms, sometimes calling us to stillness, other times pushing us into motion.

Some seasons of motherhood require us to anchor in place, slow down, go deep, and focus inward. Others invite us to sail full speed ahead, exploring, growing, and expanding. Neither is better. Both are necessary.

Motherhood is a constant ebb and flow, so some seasons will require more focus on family, while others will allow more space for personal growth. And that's okay. The key is learning to move with the tides instead of fighting against them. But motherhood has a way of humbling even the best planners.

And here's the hard truth that many of us don't want to say out loud:

I have to put myself first.

Sorry, not sorry.

Not in a selfish, dismissive way but in an intentional way. Because if I don't take care of myself, I can't take care of everyone else.

And here's the thing: as women, we are so often taught to serve, to sacrifice, to carry it all. We glorify martyrdom and call it love. But it's time we redefine what love looks like, and sometimes, that starts with giving ourselves the same care we give everyone else.

We'll dive even deeper into this in the next chapter, but for now, just know this:

Prioritizing yourself isn't selfish. It's essential.

If you're feeling stretched thin, take a breath and ask yourself:

Am I in an ebb or a flow season?

- Ebb: A time to pull back, rest, restore. (Think: newborn stage, burnout, grief, or transition.)
- **Flow:** A time to expand, create, take action. (Think: starting a project, feeling energized, getting your groove back.)

Am I resisting where I am?

Are you trying to hustle through a season that's asking for stillness? Or feeling guilty for wanting *more* in a season that's giving you space to grow?

What adjustments can I make to honor this season?

- Say no to extra obligations.
- Ask for help.
- Create boundaries that protect your peace.
- Let go of guilt and expectations that don't serve you.

Reflection: *Which season are you in right now? What do you need to fully embrace it?*

As you sit with that question, notice what feelings come up, especially if one of those is the feeling of guilt. It has a sneaky way of creeping in the moment we choose ourselves. But guilt is not a compass; it's often just the echo of outdated expectations.

And that brings us to something so many of us carry.

Let's touch briefly on mom guilt because there is a whole chapter dedicated to this topic coming up next. Mom guilt is an ever-present voice whispering:

- *You should be doing more.*
- *You're not present enough.*
- *You're being selfish.*

But, mama, let me remind you, your needs matter too.

When I started carving out time for *me,* whether it was a long run, a paddleboard session, or just a quiet coffee, I felt that guilt creep in. But then I asked myself: *Would I ever want my children to feel guilty for taking care of themselves?*

No way.

So, if I want to raise resilient, self-aware, awesome humans, I need to model what that looks like.

Motherhood isn't about mastering the tides; it's about learning to move with them.

Some days, you'll be riding high. Other days, you'll be curled up on the couch with dry shampoo in your hair and someone else's snack in your pocket.

Either way, you're doing great.

As we ride the waves of motherhood with more awareness, flexibility, and grace, we begin to realize something powerful: every *yes* we say, whether to commitments, people, or opportunities, costs us time, energy, and presence. And when we've done the work of tuning into our own compass, of letting go of guilt and embracing flow, we gain the clarity to make decisions that *actually serve us.* That's where boundaries come in, not as sea walls to keep the waves from crashing over us, but as anchors to keep us from drifting off course.

For so many of us, *no* is one of the hardest words to say. We're conditioned to be helpers, nurturers, doers, the ones who hold it all together. We say yes out of obligation, guilt, or the fear of disappointing others. We convince ourselves that we *should* be able to handle everything, that we *should* be available, that we *should* be able to juggle all the things.

But here's the truth: Every time you say yes to something that doesn't align with your priorities, you're saying no to something that does.

In the next chapter, we'll explore the art of saying no and just as importantly, how to say yes to what truly matters. Let this be your next step toward honoring your energy, protecting your peace, and living in harmony with the values you've worked so hard to define.

Chapter 4

The Art of Saying No (and Saying Yes to What Matters)

There's a moment, after you've learned to ride the waves of motherhood, when you realize: You can't ride every wave.

Some waves look exciting but lead to burnout.
Some look like opportunities but pull you away from your priorities.
Some feel like obligations, and guilt convinces you to paddle out anyway.

But here's the truth, Mermaid Mama: You don't have to catch every wave to live a full, beautiful, meaningful life. In fact, *saying no* is one of the most powerful tools we have to protect our energy, our values, and our sanity. It's not about being difficult; it's about being intentional.

If chapter 3 was about learning to flow, this chapter is about knowing when to pause. To choose stillness over the swirl of busyness. To honor your own capacity. To say *yes* only to what aligns.

And for many of us? That starts with releasing the fear of disappointing others and letting go of the guilt that's kept us overcommitted and overwhelmed.

As women, and especially as mothers, we're often conditioned to equate love with sacrifice. We're praised for being selfless, agreeable, and endlessly accommodating. Somewhere along the way, many of us internalize the belief that saying yes equals love and saying no equals letting people down.

So, when we protect our time, say no, or even prioritize joy, it feels wrong, even when it's *so right*.

But here's the truth: Again, you're rejecting what aligns with your priorities, your values, when you agree to what doesn't. And that trade-off is costly—94% of moms report feeling some level of mom guilt, with working moms feeling it most intensely.[8]

We feel guilty for:

- Wanting alone time.
- Not enjoying every moment.
- Having personal goals.
- Saying no to things we "should" do.
- Feeling burned out.

It's the invisible weight that so many working moms carry, sometimes without even realizing it.

The guilt of leaving our kids to go to work.
The guilt of not being "available" enough for our jobs.
The guilt of craving personal fulfillment outside of motherhood.
The guilt of missing moments.
The guilt of feeling like we should be "doing more."

Guilt whispers that we're never enough. That we should be giving more at work, more at home, more to our kids, our partners, our responsibilities.

And let's be honest, it's exhausting.

I've felt this guilt in every stage of my motherhood and career journey. When I was pushing myself hard at work, I felt guilty for not being more present at home. When I prioritized my kids, I felt guilty for not giving my career more attention. It felt like no matter what choice I made, something was always falling short.

---

8 Mindful Return. (n.d.). ***Mom Guilt: Why Working Moms Feel It and What to Do About It***. Retrieved from https://www.mindfulreturn.com/mom-guilt/

But here's what I've learned:

Guilt doesn't mean you're doing something wrong. It means you care.
And caring is not a bad thing. But carrying guilt every day is.
Because guilt doesn't make us better moms.
Guilt doesn't make us better employees or entrepreneurs.
Guilt doesn't make us more present; it just makes us feel weighed down, stretched thin, and never quite good enough.

It's time to break up with guilt and redefine what it means to thrive as a working mom without the constant feeling that we're failing somewhere along the way.

Being a twin mom, I've experienced so many feelings of guilt. When both babies cry at the same time, my instinct is to split myself in two. I used to feel like I was failing one of them, no matter how hard I tried.

That guilt showed up during quiet morning runs when I was training for the NYC Half Marathon and was choosing self-care over being home for early morning wakeups. It echoed when I left a high-pressure job that no longer served me, even though it "looked good" on paper. It whispered that I should be grateful always, especially because I never struggled with infertility, so how dare I ever feel overwhelmed?

Mom guilt doesn't just appear out of nowhere. It's deeply ingrained in our upbringing, in our culture, in the unspoken expectations placed on women.

Here are some of the most common guilt triggers:

- The "Perfect Mother" Myth: Society glorifies the idea of the self-sacrificing mother, always available, always giving, always putting herself last. If we don't fit this impossible mold, we feel guilty.

- Unrealistic Work Expectations: Many of us were raised to believe that success = long hours and full dedication to our careers. But when motherhood shifts our priorities, we feel guilty for not pushing as hard as we once did.

- Comparisons to Other Moms: Social media shows us "highlight reels" of other moms who seem to be *doing it all,* and we feel guilty when we struggle just to keep up.
- Feeling Like We're Always Failing at One Thing: When we're succeeding at work, we feel guilty for not being home. When we're focusing on family, we feel guilty for not doing enough at work. It's a cycle that never ends—unless we choose to step out of it.

The good news? Guilt is not a requirement of motherhood.

We have the power to rewrite the script.

I used to be the queen of overcommitting. If someone needed help, I was there. If an opportunity came up, I'd say yes, even if I had zero bandwidth. I didn't want to disappoint anyone. I wanted to be seen as capable, generous, involved.

But behind that shiny exterior was a woman who was exhausted, overwhelmed, and slowly losing touch with what she actually wanted.

Eventually, I realized I was spending so much time being everything for everyone else that I was no longer being true to myself.

However, here's what I've learned:

Guilt is often a sign that we're stepping outside of an outdated version of ourselves, one that was trained to believe sacrifice equals worthiness.

Guilt is an emotional signal. It's that inner voice that tells us we've done something wrong or at least, that we've strayed from what we believe we *should* be doing. In small doses, guilt can be useful. It tells us we may have done something wrong, or at least that our actions don't align with what we truly believe is right. But for so many mothers, guilt isn't a gentle nudge; it's a constant companion. One that nags us when we go to work, when we take a break, when we choose ourselves.

And closely tied to guilt is shame.

Guilt says, "I did something wrong."

Shame says, "I am something wrong."

While guilt can occasionally be productive, shame rarely is. Shame isolates us, disconnects us from others, and makes us feel like we're never enough, no matter how much we do. And sadly, shame doesn't just live inside us. It often seeps out, especially when we're overwhelmed or insecure. That's why it's so important to not only work through our own guilt but also to stop perpetuating shame in other moms.

There's no place for mom-shaming in a healthy, supportive community. Whether a mama works full time or stays home, serves gourmet meals or orders takeout, has a Pinterest-perfect Elf on the Shelf or skips it entirely, every mom is doing her best.

Let's cheer for the moms who find joy in going all out. And let's hold space for the ones keeping it simple. No guilt. No shame. Just grace.

So what do we do with all this? The guilt. The shame. The pressure to be everything to everyone.

We start by telling the truth, first to ourselves, then to each other. That we're not here to win gold stars for doing it all. That motherhood isn't a competition; it's a community. And the more we let go of the judgment (especially the kind we turn inward), the more space we create for something softer. Kinder. Freer.

And here's the powerful truth, Mermaid Mama:

You don't have to carry that guilt forever.

You don't have to live under the weight of old stories or societal expectations that were never written with your well-being in mind.

The guilt we feel isn't always about doing something wrong; it's often about doing something *different*.

Different from what our mothers did.

Different from what social media says is "good enough."

Different from the version of motherhood we once thought we had to live up to.

But that difference? That's where freedom lives.

It's in that space between who you were told to be and who you are becoming that you get to write a new story.

One rooted not in guilt, perfection, or shame but in grace, clarity, and purpose.

So, let's begin that shift together.

1. Recognize That Balance Is Unattainable

So many of us feel guilty because we think we should be balancing everything perfectly. But balance isn't realistic. Instead, it's about prioritizing what matters most in each moment.

Try This:

- Instead of thinking, *"I need to be fully present in both work and family at all times,"* reframe it to:
- *"Right now, my focus is on work. Later, my focus will be on my family. Both are important, and I don't have to do them at the same time."*

2. Release the Idea of the "Perfect Mom"

There is no perfect mom.

Read that again.

There are happy moms, present moms, strong moms, moms who show up in the best way they can. But perfect? Doesn't exist.

Try This:

- Make a list of everything you think a "good mom" should do.
- Then ask yourself: *Are these things actually true? Or are they expectations I've absorbed from society?*
- Cross out the unrealistic ones and focus on what actually matters to you.

3. Set Boundaries That Protect Your Time and Energy

One of the biggest causes of guilt? Overcommitting.

We say yes to things we don't have time for, then feel guilty when we're stretched too thin.

Try This: The "Hell Yes or No" Rule

- Before saying yes to anything, whether it's a work project, a PTA event, or an extra responsibility, ask yourself: *Is this a 'hell yes'? Or is it just an obligation?*
- If it's not something you truly want or have capacity for, say no. Without guilt.
- Your time is valuable. Protect it.

4. Stop Comparing Yourself to Other Moms

It's easy to look at other moms and think, *She's doing it better than me.*

But here's the truth: Everyone is struggling in ways you don't see.

Try This:

- The next time you catch yourself comparing, shift your mindset:

    - Instead of *"She's a better mom than me,"* say, *"She's doing what works for her, and I'm doing what works for me."*

- Remind yourself that there is no one right way to be a good mom.
- Your path is your own.

5. Focus on What Your Kids Actually Need (Not What You Think They Need)

We feel guilty about a lot of things that don't actually matter to our kids.

They don't need:

- A perfect, always-there mom.
- Pinterest lunches and color-coded schedules.
- A mom who sacrifices everything to prove her love.

What do they need?

- A mom who loves them unconditionally.
- A mom who listens when they talk.
- A mom who shows them that women can be strong, passionate, and fulfilled.

Try This:

- Write down the top 3 things you want your kids to remember about you as a mother.
- Anytime guilt creeps in, ask: *Is this guilt based on what really matters? Or is it based on an unrealistic expectation?*
- If it's the latter? Let. It. Go.

So, what does rewriting the narrative actually look like in everyday life?

It starts with shifting the internal dialogue, the way we respond to guilt when it shows up. Instead of letting it spiral into shame or self-doubt, we can learn to pause, get curious, and reframe it. Guilt doesn't have to be the enemy. In fact, it can be a powerful guide if we know how to work with it instead of against it.

Let's explore how to reframe guilt and turn it into a tool for clarity, alignment, and empowered decision-making.

The Guilt Reframe

Let's practice flipping the script:

Instead of…	**Try Saying…**
"I feel bad for taking time for myself."	"Taking time for me makes me a more present, patient, and energized mom."
"I should be able to handle it all."	"I deserve support just like everyone else."
"I'm being selfish for saying no."	"Protecting my peace is a form of love for me and my family."

Reflection Prompt: Guilt Check-In

Think about a recent moment when you felt guilty for doing something for yourself.

- What happened?
- What did the guilt sound like in your head?
- Was the guilt rooted in truth, or in old conditioning?
- If you were your best friend, what would you say to yourself?
- What permission do you need to give yourself today?

When we start to look at guilt not as a stop sign but as a signal to go inward and ask deeper questions, we unlock something powerful: discernment. Discernment is the practice of tuning into your inner wisdom and asking: *Is this guilt telling me something helpful, or is it just an echo of old conditioning?*

It's the ability to tell the difference between a true misalignment with your values and a false sense of failure created by unrealistic expectations.

Discernment helps you respond instead of react.

It allows you to make choices that are grounded in your truth, not in fear, people-pleasing, or comparison.

And discernment is what leads us into the next layer of living with intention, recognizing when to say no and when to say yes.

Not every ask, opportunity, or invitation is a bad thing.

Some yeses will expand your heart, deepen your joy, and align perfectly with your values.

But others? They're distractions in disguise—disguised as obligations, guilt trips, or "I really should..." pressures.

So how do you tell the difference?

Start by asking yourself these 3 core questions:

1. **Does this align with my values and current priorities?**
   (Think: Is this in tune with the season I'm in right now? Does it support my family, my wellness, or my career growth in a way that feels right?)

2. **Does this bring me joy, peace, or a sense of fulfillment?**
   (Or does it just drain me, stress me out, or stir resentment?)

3. **Am I saying yes out of obligation, fear, or guilt?**
   (Or because it's a genuine, excited yes?)

If you're answering "yes" to #3 but "no" to the first two... that's a red flag. It's probably a no disguised as a yes.

I remember one time I was asked to attend a family holiday gathering. It had been a hectic week, the twins weren't sleeping well, and I was running on fumes. Every part of me wanted to stay home, rest, and recharge, but I said yes anyway.

At the time, I was already juggling a full workload, barely keeping up with everything on my plate, and desperately needing a moment to just *be*. But I didn't want to disappoint anyone. I didn't want to seem like I wasn't making an effort or that I didn't care. So, I packed up the diaper bag, put on a smile, and went.

And the truth? I was completely overwhelmed.

I spent the day managing meltdowns, making small talk when I had nothing left to give, and counting the minutes until we could leave. I came home even more depleted than before, frustrated with myself for not honoring what I truly needed. Deep down, I knew I had said yes for all the wrong reasons.

That experience was a wake-up call. It showed me that every yes has a cost, and when we're not discerning with our time and energy, it's often our peace, our presence, and our well-being that pay the price.

Think of a time you said yes to something you didn't want to do. What happened?

- What was the cost to your energy or well-being?
- What would you do differently now?

Let's be real: saying no doesn't always come naturally, especially when you're someone who cares deeply, wants to help, and has a long history of being the "yes" person. Personally, saying no was hard for me because I equated *no* with failure, rejection, or letting someone down.

But learning to say no isn't about becoming cold or closed off.
It's about becoming clear and connected to what matters most.

It's about honoring your values, energy, and capacity, especially in seasons where you're already stretched thin.

You don't have to say yes just because you can.
And believe it or not, you can say no and still be kind.
You can say no and still be supportive.
You can say no and still be you.

The Guilt-Free "No" Framework

Here's a simple 3-part approach to help you say no with clarity and kindness:

1. **Acknowledge the ask with gratitude or empathy.**
   (e.g., "Thank you so much for thinking of me…" or "I really appreciate you reaching out…")
2. **State your boundary clearly and confidently.**
   (e.g., "I'm not able to take that on right now…")
3. **Optional: Offer a soft landing or alternative (if it feels right).**
   (e.g., "I'd be happy to help another time…" or "Here's another resource that might help…")

Now that you have the framework, let's bring it to life with a few real-world examples because sometimes the hardest part is finding the right words.

Guilt-Free "No" Scripts

Let these be your starting point, but feel free to tweak them to make them your own.

The Simple No

"Thanks for thinking of me, but I won't be able to take that on right now."

The No with Gratitude

"I'm honored you asked! I'm in a season of focusing more on family right now, so I'll have to pass."

The Soft No with Options

"I can't commit fully to that, but I'd be happy to offer input via email if that helps."

The Firm Boundary

"I've made a commitment to protect my evenings for family and rest, so I won't be available after 6 p.m."

Practice Exercise: Write Your Own "No" Script

Use this space to craft a few "no" phrases you can return to anytime:

My Default No:

My Work-Life Boundary No:

My Family or Friend No (with love):

Bonus: The Pause Strategy

You don't have to give an answer *on the spot*. If you feel yourself slipping into auto-yes mode, try saying:

- "Let me check in with my schedule and get back to you."
- "I want to make sure I can give this the attention it deserves, so can I follow up tomorrow?"
- "Thanks for thinking of me! I need a little space to see what's realistic right now."

Giving yourself a moment to breathe helps you respond from your compass, not from guilt or pressure.

Guilt may show up. That doesn't mean it has to lead your choices. You are allowed to live a life that's nourishing for you, not just one that looks good on the outside or pleases everyone else.

Let this chapter be your permission slip:

- To pause.
- To say no.
- To prioritize joy.
- To choose rest.
- To trust your own compass.

You deserve a life of peace, connection, and meaning, not just survival. And when you take care of yourself, you're not just surviving motherhood, you're showing your kids how to thrive in their own lives, too. When your children see you honor your limits, ask for help, and choose joy over burn-out, you're giving them permission to do the same.

And part of that modeling? Releasing the myth that you have to do it all alone.

Letting go of unrealistic expectations opens the door to delegation, support, and shared responsibility. When you release the pressure to do it all perfectly, you create space for what truly matters and for the people around you to step in and support you.

Let's talk about what that actually looks like.

Delegation and Asking for Help—You Don't Have to Do It All

Repeat after me: "I do not have to do everything myself."

Asking for help is not a weakness. Delegating tasks does not mean you're failing. Saying no to something doesn't mean you aren't capable; it means you are prioritizing what actually deserves your energy.

Ways to Lighten Your Load:

At Home: Let your partner take on more responsibilities. Teach your kids to help. Order groceries online instead of spending hours at the store.

At Work: Ask for extensions when needed. Speak up when your workload is too much. Delegate tasks to coworkers when possible.

With Friends and Family: Let go of the pressure to always be available. It's okay to not answer texts right away. It's okay to say no to plans when you need a break.

Journal Prompts:

- *Where in my life do I need to ask for more help?*
- *What tasks or responsibilities can I delegate or let go of?*

Mama, you are doing enough. You are showing up. You are loving your kids and building a life that works for you.

And that? That's more than enough.

So let's say goodbye to guilt and start embracing the truth:

You can thrive at work and at home.

You can be a great mom and chase your dreams.

You do not have to prove your love by sacrificing yourself.

You are already doing an incredible job.

Saying no isn't about shutting people out; it's about protecting your time, energy, and well-being so you can show up fully for what truly matters.

Let go of the guilt. Embrace the power of your NO. And trust that by saying no to what drains you, you are saying YES to what makes your life richer, fuller, and more aligned with who you truly are.

Now that we've created the space by clearing the clutter of guilt and obligation, it's time to fill it with something so often forgotten in adulthood: joy.

Because once you've said no to what drains you, you're free to say a wholehearted YES to what lights you up.

In the next chapter, we dive into the power of play, creativity, and fun, not just for your kids but for you. Get ready to rediscover what it means to feel alive again, mermaid-style.

Chapter 5

Embracing Play and Joy: Why Moms Deserve Fun Too

Motherhood is serious business. From the moment we wake up (usually before we even want to), we're managing schedules, wiping noses, making sure everyone is fed, dressed, and somewhat functioning. Our days are filled with responsibilities, decisions, and a constant mental load that never seems to let up.

But in the midst of all this doing, we often forget what it feels like to just be. To be light. To be silly. To be playful.

That's where joy comes in, not as a reward for finishing the to-do list but as a lifeline woven into our daily lives.

But let me ask you something: When was the last time you truly played?

Not just watched your kids play. Not just supervised an activity. Not just checked something off the list because it was "good for them."

When was the last time you let yourself be fully immersed in joy, in the moment, in something fun just for YOU?

For a long time, I didn't think play was for me. Play was for kids. Play was for people who had time, people who didn't have a million responsibilities to juggle. I convinced myself that having fun was something that had to be earned, something I could only do after everything else was done.

I told myself things like:

- *I don't have time for that.*
- *There are more important things to do.*
- *I'd feel silly.*
- *I don't even know what I'd do for fun anymore.*

But here's the reality: joy is not a luxury. It's a mental health necessity.

Just like we need food, sleep, and connection, we also need joy, creativity, laughter, and play to thrive. According to the National Institute of Play, incorporating play into adult life can increase adaptability, reduce stress-related illnesses, and even improve long-term memory.[9]

And yet, joy is often treated like a luxury instead of a necessity, especially in motherhood.

Somewhere along the way, I convinced myself I needed permission to play. As a child, I often felt too tall, too grown-up, too responsible to join in the carefree joy of being a kid. I was expected to sit with the adults, to act older than my years. Play was something I watched from the sidelines. And yet, something inside me longed to be set free. I resisted and resisted, dipping only the tiniest toe (or fin) into the waters of whimsy.

But now? Now that I have children of my own, play is at the forefront. I don't know why I was waiting for someone to give me permission, but I realize now that I don't need it. I can and will embrace both work and play. I will be the woman who dreams big and gets things done. The mother who nurtures, and the professional who builds, the mermaid who swims between all these worlds with joy. I can work hard and still splash in the waves.

There's a unique magic that happens when we let ourselves play. Not just facilitate it, supervise it, or schedule it—but actually participate in it. To move, to laugh, to feel fully immersed in joy. That kind of alignment is where creativity thrives. Where soul and purpose intertwine.

---

9 National Institute for Play. (n.d.). ***Why play matters***. https://www.nifplay.org/why-play-matters/

And here's why this matters: a 2022 survey by Motherly found that 93% of mothers reported feeling burned out at least occasionally, with over 50% saying they feel this way frequently.[10]

In a world that glorifies hustle, choosing play isn't frivolous; it's revolutionary.

It's easy to dismiss play as something optional, something for when everything else is done. But what if play is actually one of the most important tools we have, not just for feeling better but for living better?

The Joy-Creativity Connection

This is where the magic of joy truly shows up.

When I walk or run, something shifts inside me. I come up with new ideas, solve problems, and connect dots that felt scattered before. Movement is medicine, but it's also creative fuel.

In fact, a Stanford University study found that walking increases creative output by 60%.[11]

That means your joy isn't just healing; it's wildly productive. It unlocks clarity, innovation, and energy. And that counts, especially in motherhood, where creative problem-solving is a daily reality.

So if you've ever thought play was indulgent, think again. Play is powerful. It helps you show up as the visionary, intuitive, and resilient version of yourself.

Now that we've talked about why joy matters, let's talk about how to actually bring more of it into your day. Because play doesn't just happen, we have to make room for it, even if it's just a few moments at a time.

---

10 Motherly. (2022). ***State of Motherhood Report 2022***. https://www.mother.ly/research/state-of-motherhood-2022/

11 Oppezzo, M., & Schwartz, D. L. (2014). Give your ideas some legs: The positive effect of walking on creative thinking. ***Journal of Experimental Psychology: Learning, Memory, and Cognition, 40***(4), 1142–1152. https://doi.org/10.1037/a0036577

1. Identify What Feels Fun to *You*

Think back to your childhood. What made you feel alive?

Let go of what joy "should" look like and get honest about what actually lights you up.

Journal Prompts:

- *What did I love doing as a child that I've stopped doing?*
- *What brings me joy now?*
- *What new things am I curious to try?*

2. Schedule Play (Yes, Really)

We schedule meetings, appointments, and school drop-offs, but what about fun? Play deserves a place on your calendar.

Try:

- A weekly "fun date" with yourself or your kids
- A Play Jar of ideas like: "paint with no rules," "dance break," "try a new hobby"
- Turning chores into games (yes, it counts!)

3. Recognize When You Feel Guilty

In the chapter before this one, we talked about the weight of mom guilt and how it shows up in sneaky, persistent ways and tries to convince us that taking care of ourselves is selfish.

But here's the truth: Joy is not selfish. It's self-sustaining. Play doesn't make you less productive. It makes you more present. It allows you to refill your cup so you can pour into others from a place of wholeness, not depletion.

If guilt starts to creep in, try reframing the thought:

Guilt Thought	Reframe
"I should be doing something productive."	"Joy is productive because it fills my cup."
"I don't have time for fun."	"I make time for what matters. I matter."
"I feel silly."	"Silly is sacred. Play is powerful."

Let this be your permission slip to release the guilt and reclaim your joy—fully, freely, and without apology.

When we intentionally invite joy into our lives by identifying what lights us up, making time for it, and releasing the guilt that tries to stand in the way, we begin to shift our entire experience of motherhood and life.

But joy doesn't just live in scheduled moments or big adventures. It lives in the quiet in-between. The small rituals. The ordinary days that hold extraordinary magic, if we're paying attention.

Back in 2020, I felt something stirring in my spirit: a need to intentionally reclaim joy. The world was in chaos as the pandemic had turned our lives upside down. I was working in healthcare at the time, overwhelmed by the emotional weight of what felt like an endless crisis. I knew I needed something to hold onto. Something light. Something that reminded me I was still alive.

So I created Joyful July as a personal commitment to weave more play, presence, and pleasure into my everyday life. Each day, I posted prompts, activities, and reflections. And I was amazed at how many women joined me, craving the same thing: permission to feel joy again.

Just about every July since, I've recommitted to that promise. Not because life gets easier in the summer (spoiler alert: it doesn't) but because joy is an act of resistance. Choosing joy in a world that glorifies exhaustion is a radical kind of self-care. It says, *I'm still here—and I want to live, not just survive.*

On Day 1 of that first #JoyfulJuly2020, I sat quietly with my morning coffee in my "Off Duty Mermaid" mug, smiled at the sunshine, and reminded myself that joy doesn't need a big stage.

You don't have to wait for a vacation to have fun.

Joy lives in the little things like:

- Dancing in the kitchen while cooking (bonus points for belting out show tunes with the kids!).
- Singing at the top of your lungs in the car.
- Swimming in a mermaid tail just for fun.
- Running through the sprinklers.
- Coloring outside the lines.
- Playing tag or hide-and-seek.
- Sitting outside and playing "leaves" with your babies—which is a game where we put leaves in and out of cups.

Joy doesn't need to be big. It just needs to be yours. And the more we embrace it, the more we teach our children that life is meant to be enjoyed, not just managed.

Because at the end of the day, joy isn't something we have to earn; it's something we get to choose. In the small, imperfect, beautiful moments. In the middle of the mess. In the mundane and the magical.

So, before you move on, take a breath. Let yourself pause. And reflect on the following:

1. What did joy look like for you as a child?
2. When was the last time you felt truly playful or lighthearted?
3. What small, everyday moments bring you joy now?
4. How can you build more joy into your week—on purpose?

5. Is there a "mermaid tail" moment waiting for you—something symbolic you can do to embody your return to joy?

The most fulfilled mothers I know? They make space for fun. They laugh. They let loose. They remember that life is to be lived, not just managed.

So, Mermaid Mama, put on the tail. Splash in the waves. Dance like nobody's watching. Your joy is your strength.

A Note on Grief and Growth

No one told me that motherhood would involve so much grieving.

Not just the heartbreaking grief we associate with loss but the subtle, slow-burning kind. The kind that creeps in when you're rocking a baby at 3 a.m. and realizing your freedom, your time, your career identity, whatever it was before, has shifted forever. The kind that stirs when your children grow out of a stage you swore you'd never survive... and you find yourself missing it anyway.

We talk a lot about the love, the joy, the pride. But we don't always talk about the sadness that tags along, quietly.

We grieve the version of ourselves that existed before motherhood.
We grieve the friendships that faded when life got busy.
We grieve the spontaneity, the space, the dreams we shelved.
We grieve expectations that didn't match our reality.
We even grieve parts of motherhood itself as each season ends.
It's okay to feel this way. It doesn't make you ungrateful. It makes you human.

Dr. Earl A. Grollman says, "Grief is not a disorder, a disease or a sign of weakness. It is an emotional, physical and spiritual necessity, the price you pay for love."[12]

---

12 Grollman, E. A. (2014). *Straight talk about death for teenagers: How to cope with losing someone you love* (p. 6). Beacon Press

Ignoring grief doesn't make it go away; it buries it. And buried grief becomes burnout, irritability, or numbness. When we allow ourselves to name the grief, we begin to release it. And in that release, we make space for healing and joy to return.

Research supports this need for acknowledgment. A study in the *Journal of Affective Disorders* found that nearly one in five women experience postpartum depression, often exacerbated by feelings of loss and identity confusion.[13]

You are not alone in mourning who you used to be.

That version of you, full of ambition, spontaneity, independence, or simply routine, still matters. She paved the way for the woman you are today. And while motherhood may have reshaped your days, it didn't erase her. She's still within you, just expressed in new and quieter ways.

So take a moment. Write a letter to your pre-motherhood self. Thank her. Grieve her. And then acknowledge all the ways she still lives on in who you are now.

You can also try these prompts in your journal:

- *What have I let go of since becoming a mother?*
- *What am I grieving that I haven't given myself permission to feel?*
- *What new parts of myself have I discovered through this process?*

This is the duality of motherhood: grief and gratitude, side by side. One doesn't cancel out the other; they coexist.

As we wrap Part 1 of your journey, I want you to pause and honor all the work you've done to reclaim space for yourself. The boundaries you've drawn. The grace you've extended. The play you've embraced.

Because the next part? It's about expansion.

---

13 Shorey, S., Chee, C. Y. I., Ng, E. D., Chan, Y. H., Tam, W. W. S., & Chong, Y. S. (2018). Prevalence and incidence of postpartum depression among healthy mothers: A systematic review and meta-analysis. *Journal of Psychiatric Research, 104*, 235–248. https://doi.org/10.1016/j.jpsychires.2018.08.001

It's about using the joy you've cultivated to show up with more intention in your:

- Home
- Parenting
- Partnerships
- Career
- Community

We don't serve others by sacrificing ourselves. We serve best when we are whole.

Motherhood isn't just about caring for ourselves; it's also about nurturing, guiding, and showing up for those we love. We are caregivers, partners, mentors, and leaders, whether it's within our families, friendships, careers, or communities.

But here's the thing: You can't pour from an empty cup.

That's why Part 1 of this book was all about taking care of yourself first, not because your needs matter more than others' but because when you are strong, fulfilled, and aligned, you can give from a place of abundance instead of exhaustion.

We laid the foundation for what it means to live in alignment with your Mermaid Mama Compass, ensuring that you are cared for, fulfilled, and anchored in your purpose.

But our impact doesn't stop with us. The work we do within ourselves naturally expands outward, shaping the way we show up in our families, careers, and communities.

Now, as we move into Part 2, we'll explore how to extend that care and intention beyond ourselves, to our children, our partners, our workplaces, and the larger world we influence.

And now that we've awakened your inner mermaid, it's time to let her swim deeper. In Part 2, we'll explore:

- Creating a home that fosters growth and trust
- Raising confident, resilient children while still honoring your dreams
- Strengthening your most important relationships
- Aligning your career with your values

You're not just managing motherhood. You're shaping a life and a legacy.

Let's keep swimming.

Part 2:

Expanding Our Impact—Family, Career, and Community

If there's one thing I know for sure, it's this:

Mothers are leaders.

Whether we realize it or not, we are constantly leading—in our homes, our careers, our friendships, and our communities. The energy we bring into our spaces shapes the people around us. The values we live by influence our children. The decisions we make in our careers, businesses, and volunteer work have a ripple effect that extends far beyond what we can see.

That's why Part 1 of this book focused on you, because before we can take care of others, we must take care of ourselves.

Now, as we move into Part 2, we're shifting the focus outward.

This section is about how we take what we've built within ourselves, our confidence, our clarity, our well-being, and use it to show up as intentional, empowered leaders in our families, our careers, and our communities.

It's about learning how to:

- Create a home of connection and love.
- Nurture a strong partnership while raising confident, resilient kids.
- Strengthen your support system through authentic friendships and community connections.
- Build a career or business that aligns with your values—and your family life.

But let's be real: this isn't easy.

As women, we are often expected to do it all, to be the perfect mom, the loving partner, the high-achieving professional, the friend who never drops the ball. And we often carry guilt when we feel like we're not doing enough in any of these areas.

But here's what I want you to remember: Leading your family, career, and community doesn't mean doing everything perfectly. It means showing up with intention, clarity, and purpose.

The Myth of "Having It All"

For years, we've been fed the idea that we should be able to "have it all." A thriving career, a Pinterest-worthy home, a picture-perfect family life, a body that bounces back after babies, a social life that never suffers, and the ability to juggle it all without breaking a sweat.

But trying to have it all at once is a fast track to burnout.

This isn't about doing everything equally. It's about making intentional choices about where to focus your energy in each season of life. Some seasons will require more presence at home. Some will give you the space to pour into your career. Some will call you to expand outward into leadership, activism, or community work.

The key is to stop measuring success by how much you're juggling and start measuring it by how aligned you feel in the areas that matter most.

You don't have to do it all.

But you do have to choose what matters most in each season and honor that choice without guilt.

Clarity doesn't always come in a quiet moment. Sometimes it arrives in the chaos. In the blur of bottle feeds, deadlines, and family group texts, I've had to pause and ask: *What actually matters right now?*

And the answer isn't always the same.

During the first year with our twins, my priorities were survival and bonding. I gave myself permission to say no to extra work, to pass on social events, and to let things be "good enough" at home. Other seasons have been filled with creative energy, where I could write, coach, launch new projects, and stretch outward. Still others required me to pull back and rest, to let healing be the priority.

What matters most is fluid, not fixed. The real power is in the choosing.

I remember one evening during that first year of motherhood when the weight of everything felt especially heavy. The twins were both sick, I had looming deadlines, and the house looked like a tornado had passed through. I stood in the kitchen, staring at a sink full of dishes and a floor covered in toys, fighting back tears, not because of one big thing but because of everything all at once. I knew I needed a reset.

So I took a breath and asked myself: *How do I want to feel right now? What do my kids need most right now? What can wait?*

After thinking about what I needed at that time, I gave myself permission to step back. I paused a few work projects, said no to things I might've said yes to out of obligation, and gave myself grace to just *be*. I swapped productivity for presence, leaned into slow afternoons with the boys, and let cuddles count as accomplishments.

It wasn't polished or perfect, but it felt like peace.

Choosing what matters most isn't about abandoning your ambition or giving up on anything. It's about honoring your capacity and leading your life with intention.

And that, at its core, is what leadership truly is.

Because leadership isn't just about titles or visibility; it's about how you show up in the world, especially when no one's watching. It's in the quiet decisions, the daily choices, the way you care for others and yourself.

When we think about leadership, we often picture CEOs, activists, or public figures. But leadership doesn't have to look like standing on a stage or running a company.

Leadership starts right where you are.

In your home, you are a leader. Every time you model emotional regulation, communicate with compassion, or set a boundary rooted in love, you are leading. You're shaping the culture of your home, the values of your children, and the story of your family.

And when you choose what matters most in your current season, you give others permission to do the same. You lead by example, not perfection.

So whether you're navigating diaper changes or board meetings, know this: You're leading. And it matters.

In your home, you are a leader.

- You are shaping the next generation through the way you love, communicate, and show up.
- You are leading by example, showing your children what it

means to be strong, kind, and resilient.

- You are making decisions every day that impact the emotional and physical well-being of your family.

In your career, you are a leader.

- Whether you're running a business, climbing the corporate ladder, or finding harmony between work and family, your voice matters.
- The way you set boundaries, advocate for yourself, and make choices that align with your values sets the tone for the people around you.
- If you own a business, work in leadership, or have a platform, you have an opportunity to use your influence for positive change.

In your community, you are a leader.

- Whether it's through volunteering, mentoring, or simply being someone who uplifts and supports other women, you are creating ripples of impact.
- Small actions like helping a fellow mom, standing up for a cause you believe in, or leading with kindness create waves bigger than you know.

You don't have to choose between being a present mother, a successful professional, or an engaged community member. But you do have to decide how to navigate these roles in a way that aligns with your values and energy in each season of life.

We're going to talk about the real-life challenges of managing it all. The messy parts, the growing pains, and the moments of doubt. But more importantly, we're going to focus on how you can build a life that is not just busy but fulfilling, intentional, and deeply aligned with what matters most to you.

Part 2 is where the inner work turns outward, where the values you've reconnected with start shaping the world around you. This section is about how you bring your whole self, your strength, softness, creativity, and clarity, into the spaces where you lead and love.

And that begins with the space closest to you: your home.

Before we dive into systems, schedules, and strategies, let's first talk about the physical and emotional environments we live in every day. The spaces where we wake up, work, gather, and rest. Because those spaces and the atmosphere we create have the power to either support or stifle everything we're building.

Chapter 6

Designing Your Lagoon: Crafting Intentional Spaces for Connection, Creativity, and Calm

Your environment isn't just where life happens. It shapes how life feels. And before we can build a strong, connected family, we must first create the environment that supports connection. The space we inhabit—the physical corners of our home, the desks where we dream, the cozy nooks where we reflect—sets the tone for how we show up in our lives.

As Mermaid Mamas, our spaces can become more than just rooms filled with things. They can become our lagoons: restorative sanctuaries that reflect our values, recharge our energy, and invite joy, clarity, and alignment.

That sanctuary doesn't have to be picture-perfect; it just has to feel like home.

Right now, the twins' playpen is my new favorite place. It feels like the heart of the house. It's not fancy. It's not curated for Pinterest. But it's real. It's where all of us have napped at least once, curled up in a sunbeam or sprawled out after a chaotic morning. It's where giggles echo, books tumble, and time seems to slow just enough to remind me of what truly matters.

That space, in all its beautiful mess, has become our shared sanctuary.

And yet, I didn't always see it that way.

I used to daydream about the perfect space, waiting and wanting to create the ideal nook, the serene corner untouched by snack dust and rogue golf balls. A room free of magnets, blocks, and the ever-growing collection of boy-house chaos. A sacred, tidy space where I could write, breathe, and just be.

Eventually, I stopped waiting for perfect and started carving out something real. I created my own little corner, tucked near a window, surrounded by plants, bathed in sunlight, with my favorite candle lit nearby. It offers a view of the trees and is a breath of calm in the midst of our family's joyful chaos. It's nowhere near flawless or pristine, but it's mine. And in that space, I feel a little more grounded, a little more connected to myself.

That's the beauty of designing your own lagoon: It doesn't have to be magazine-worthy. It just has to feel like you.

And as it turns out, this instinct to create a nourishing space isn't just a personal preference; it's backed by science.

We often think of wellness as something we cultivate internally, through food, mindset, or movement, but the spaces we spend our time in have a profound influence on our emotional and mental well-being. Research backs this up: a study published in *Personality and Social Psychology Bulletin* found that people with cluttered homes tend to have higher levels of cortisol, the stress hormone, and are more likely to experience fatigue and depression.[14]

Our environment either grounds us or grates against us. And while the ideal space may always be a work in progress, it's possible to carve out pockets of peace, even in the busiest seasons of motherhood.

And when it comes to creativity and focus? A well-designed environment can make all the difference.

---

14 Saxbe, D. E., & Repetti, R. L. (2009). No place like home: Home tours correlate with daily patterns of mood and cortisol. ***Personality and Social Psychology Bulletin, 36***(1), 71–81. https://doi.org/10.1177/0146167209352864

So how do we create our own personal lagoon?

1. Define Your Lagoon's Purpose

Before bringing in decor or lighting, get clear on the function of your space. Ask yourself:

- *What do I want this space to help me feel or do?*
- *Is it a space to retreat and recharge? To brainstorm and create? To reconnect with my family?*

Your answers will guide the design. Here are a few types of lagoons you might consider:

- The Creative Lagoon: A space filled with journals, a vision board, paints, or a whiteboard. Bright colors and inspiring quotes spark new ideas.
- The Relaxation Lagoon: A cozy nook with soft blankets, calming scents, and dim lighting. Think candles, essential oils, and gentle textures.
- The Professional Lagoon: A clean, minimalist workspace with streamlined tools and reduced distractions. A sanctuary for productivity.
- The Connection Lagoon: A warm, inviting space where you gather as a family, free of screens and rich with presence.

2. Anchor the Space with Wellness Elements

Your lagoon should support your whole self—mind, body, and soul. Here are a few elements to weave in:

- Natural Light: Position your space near a window or use lighting that mimics daylight. Exposure to natural light is proven to improve mood, sleep, and focus.

- Nature-Inspired Decor: Bring in oceanic elements like seashells, sea glass, driftwood, or indoor plants and add a small tabletop fountain for calming energy.
- Color Cues: Use blues and greens for calm, yellows and oranges for creative fire. Let your palette reflect your purpose.

3. Declutter and Organize

Clutter drains our energy and fogs our focus. Take time to remove what no longer serves you. Use baskets, shelves, or under-desk storage to keep things tidy.

4. Personalize with Meaning

Make your lagoon feel like you. Add elements that ground and uplift you:

- Family photos or artwork that brings you joy
- A vision board of your dreams and goals
- Books that have shaped you
- Mermaid tokens like ocean art, sea-inspired candles, or meaningful shells

Let it tell your story.

5. Design for Flexibility

Your lagoon should evolve just as you do. Maybe this season, it's a space for yoga and journaling. In the next, it becomes a reading nook or a Zoom call sanctuary.

Use flexible furniture, rolling carts, and movable décor to let your space shift with your needs.

6. Build in Wellness Rituals

Infuse your daily rhythm into your space:

- A yoga mat tucked in the corner
- A diffuser with your favorite essential oils or your favorite candle
- A shelf with herbal teas or a self-care jar filled with encouraging notes
- A "no phones allowed" zone to promote presence

Your lagoon becomes a place where wellness isn't something you have to remember. It's something that lives in your environment.

7. Evaluate and Refresh

Once you've created your space, give yourself permission to refresh and adjust as often as needed.

- Does it feel energizing and peaceful?
- Is it serving your goals and rhythms?
- Could a small shift make it feel more aligned?

Let your lagoon be a living space, a mirror of your evolution, not a fixed destination.

Real-Life Lagoon Inspiration

To spark your imagination, here are a few lagoon ideas:

- The Zen Writer's Nook: A reading chair, string lights, a salt lamp, and a stack of ocean-poetry books for the mama who needs to carve out a corner of calm in a bustling household.
- The Mompreneur's Command Center: With a sleek desk, whiteboard calendar, framed affirmations, and her kids' artwork lining the shelves, this mama is equal parts business and heart.

- The Mermaid Mama Retreat: A beach-themed corner with sandy-beige textiles, ocean soundscapes, and a glass jar of collected seashells are this mama's reminder that she's always connected to the sea within.

Creating an intentional space isn't just about aesthetics; it's about energy. It's about surrounding yourself with the reminders of who you are and what you're becoming. It's about designing a space that holds you as you mother, dream, and grow. Because when you are supported by your environment, you show up more grounded, more connected, and more alive, for yourself, for your family, and for the world.

So dive in. Light the candle. Fluff the pillow. Hang the art. Build your lagoon and let it be your sacred space for who you are growing into.

But even the most serene lagoon isn't meant to be a solitary place.

It's also where connection happens, where stories are shared, laughter echoes, and love takes root in the everyday moments. Once you've created a space that nurtures your soul, the next step is to fill it with intention, trust, and togetherness.

Because a home isn't just walls and furniture—it's the heartbeat of your family.

Chapter 7

The Heart of the Lagoon: Building a Strong, Connected Family

Every lagoon has a heart, a still, sacred center where the waters are calm and life thrives. In our lives, that heart is often our family. It's the space we come back to when the world feels overwhelming. It's the place where we root ourselves in love, security, and belonging.

But building a strong and connected family doesn't just happen. It's not a default setting; it's an ongoing practice. A conscious choice. A daily return to presence. And that practice begins the moment we step into the role of parent.

When I became a mother, I expected a lot of other things.
Sleepless nights? Check.
The overwhelming love everyone talks about? Absolutely.
The constant juggling act of keeping tiny humans alive while also attempting to have a career, pursue personal dreams, and manage a somewhat functional household? Oh yeah, that was a given.

What I didn't expect was how much motherhood would force me to confront my own past and how it would make me reflect deeply on my childhood, my family, and the unresolved feelings I had quietly carried for years.

I knew I wanted to build a strong, loving, connected family and a home that felt real.

But what did that even mean? What does that look like when your own experience of family is complicated to say the least? How do you lay a solid foundation when parts of your own feel fractured?

For a long time, I struggled with the idea of home.

My parents divorced when I was young, and I didn't fully understand how much that shaped me until I had children of my own. Family felt fragile, like something that could shift or break at any moment. I carried that feeling with me for years, never realizing how much it influenced my own beliefs about relationships, stability, and what it meant to create a home. We also moved a lot when I was younger. It felt like just when I was starting to settle into a new house, everything would change again. This constant movement taught me how to adapt, how to be extremely flexible, but it also taught me how to hold back a little, just in case things didn't last.

And then, suddenly, I had a family of my own. Not just as a recent twin mother but as a stepmother too.

Becoming a stepmom has been one of the most unexpected, humbling roles of my life.

Unlike biological parenting, where bonds begin from birth, stepparenting begins in the middle of someone else's story. There are no guarantees of affection or acceptance. You don't just show up and become family; you have to build it, gently and with great patience.

For me, the biggest challenge was figuring out where I fit in and to learn how to be a loving, supportive presence without overstepping boundaries.

One of the biggest lessons I've learned as a stepmom is that family isn't defined by DNA. It's defined by showing up, again and again, in ways that matter.

That means:

- Letting relationships unfold naturally, without rushing the process.

- Respecting their history and the bonds they already have.
- Understanding that love in blended families can look different, and that's okay.

I wanted so badly for my stepkids to feel comfortable with me, to trust me, to see me as a positive force in their lives. But I had to accept that trust and love aren't things you can force—they have to be built over time.

In many ways, stepmotherhood is an exercise in holding steady in the background while still being fully present. And that in itself teaches kids so much about what real, unconditional support looks like.

But even quiet presence requires deep emotional work.

I found myself blending into the lives of children who had already established rhythms, routines, and relationships long before I arrived. And the questions about family only deepened when the twins arrived.

No longer just figuring out what *I* needed, I was now responsible for creating a foundation for all of us. For shaping what "home" would mean not just for my biological children but also for my stepchildren.

When I first met the boys, I had to learn how to hold space without overstepping, how to support without trying to replace. It was a delicate dance of love and patience, and one I was still figuring out when the twins arrived.

Suddenly, I wasn't just a stepmom navigating someone else's story; I was also a new mother, responsible for shaping the stories of two new babies. In many ways, the timeline of our family didn't unfold in a straight line. We came together in layers, through time, trust, and the slow building of something real.

Here's what I've come to understand: family isn't about getting it right all the time.

It's about being present.

It's about showing up, again and again, even when it's hard and you don't have all the answers. Even when it's messy. Especially when it's messy.

It's about creating a space where love, security, and connection are stronger than the inevitable conflicts and challenges that arise.

It's about deciding that even if the version of family you grew up with wasn't perfect, you have the power to create something different.

According to a 2021 report from the Search Institute, strong family relationships are one of the most powerful predictors of a child's long-term success and well-being, including academic achievement, mental health, and resilience.[15] The single most important factor? Feeling connected and supported at home.

This means our presence matters more than our perfection.

It means that the version of family you grew up with doesn't have to be the one you pass down. You get to decide what home means now, and that's incredibly empowering.

I keep returning to the metaphor of the lagoon when thinking about the concept of what home means to me now: a safe, protected space teeming with life, full of movement, always shifting but still whole.

A lagoon isn't static. It ebbs and flows. Sometimes it's pristine and serene, other times murky and wild. Family is the same way.

But at its core, it is a place of belonging.

That's what I want for my family: not perfection, not control, just belonging.

A space where my kids feel secure, seen, and deeply loved.

And let me be clear: very rarely has our home been pristine. There are toys scattered across the floor, baby wipes tucked into couch cushions, and the

---

15 Search Institute. (2022). *Elements of developmental relationships: A Search Institute research review*. Retrieved from https://www.search-institute.org/wp-content/uploads/2022/09/ElementsofDevelopmentalRelationships-FINAL.pdf

occasional mystery stain I still haven't identified. The pet hair drifts around the house like tumbleweeds no matter how often I vacuum.

But that chaos? It's ours. And in the middle of it, I've carved out a corner just for me. A small space filled with plants, sunlight, and a view of the outside world. It's not fancy, but it's mine. It's the one spot in the house that feels calm when everything else feels like a whirlwind. It grounds me when the mess feels overwhelming. It reminds me that I can hold both a loud, chaotic home and a quiet inner peace.

That's what I'm trying to build—not a perfect house but a soulful home.

A home where my children and stepchildren feel safe to be themselves. Where they know they are deeply loved. Where we weather the storms together.

But building that kind of family doesn't just happen. It takes intention, reflection, and a willingness to do the inner work, especially when you're carrying your own wounds from the past.

For me, becoming a mother and a stepmother brought so much of this to the surface.

One of the hardest truths about parenting is this: We don't just pass on our genes; we pass on our patterns.

The way we express affection.

How we handle conflict.

What we do with our anger or sadness.

The way we express (or withhold) love.

The way we react under stress.

How we show up (or withdraw) under pressure.

The way we communicate (or don't communicate) emotions.

So much of what we do in our own families comes from what we experienced growing up, whether we realize it or not.

A study from the Harvard Center on the Developing Child found that early childhood environments, including family emotional climate, have lasting effects on how children process stress and regulate emotions.[16] That means the emotional tone of our homes matters deeply.

And that truth hit especially hard for me.

Shortly after I moved to Florida, I went through one of the most difficult relationships of my life. The kind that leaves you questioning everything—your worth, your instincts, your ability to trust. I carried that pain with me, tucked behind my ambition and my smile, as I tried to move forward while still suffering beneath the surface.

Healing didn't happen overnight. It's still happening.

I've done a lot of work since then… deep, uncomfortable, necessary work. And sometimes, when I catch myself shutting down during conflict or trying to fix everything to avoid tension, I hear that old version of me whispering in the background. Then I have to ask myself: *Is this what I want to model?*

The answer is no.

I know that if I want to change the patterns, I have to be intentional about what I'm building. I don't want to parent on autopilot, repeating cycles I never consciously chose. I want to create a home where my kids, both biological and step, feel safe, seen, and supported in a way that is thoughtful, not just inherited.

I want my home to be a place where emotions are acknowledged, not avoided.

I want my children to feel secure, even when life gets messy.

I want my relationships to be built on honest, open communication.

---

16 National Scientific Council on the Developing Child. (2014). *Excessive stress disrupts the architecture of the developing brain* (Working Paper No. 3). Center on the Developing Child at Harvard University. https://developingchild.harvard.edu/wp-content/uploads/2024/10/Stress_Disrupts_Architecture_Developing_Brain-1.pdf

And in order to create that, I had to start doing the work on myself first.

One of the biggest lessons I've learned as a mother is that you don't just pass down your genetics, you pass down your patterns, too.

That's why family culture matters. Because without intention, we default to what we know. And if what we know isn't what we want to pass down, we have the power to change it.

This is where we shift from recognizing the past to creating the future by defining the kind of home, relationships, and values we want to cultivate.

Every family has a culture, whether we name it or not.

Some of us grew up in homes where love was expressed through quality time. Others were raised in families where acts of service or words of encouragement were the primary way love was shown.

As mothers and stepmothers, we get to decide what kind of culture we create within our own homes. A strong family culture isn't just about rules and routines, it's about values. It's about deciding what matters most to us.

In our home, our culture is built around curiosity, kindness, and play. We make space for big feelings and messy days. We value creativity over comparison. We try to model what it means to take care of each other and ourselves.

It's not about having a picture-perfect routine. It's about cultivating a rhythm that feels real.

Our home is a place where your opinion is always welcome, where talking and listening are part of the daily flow. We don't have dinner at the table every night. In fact, most nights, I'm eating the twins' leftover chicken nuggets while standing at the counter, and the older boys are coming in and out between school, work, and growing up. But even in the chaos, there's connection. We check in. We laugh. We listen to music. We hold space for each other's moods and milestones, even when they don't align.

It's flexible. It's imperfect. But it's ours.

And at the heart of it all is this shared understanding: We are here for one another.

Creating that kind of family culture doesn't require a perfect schedule or matching pajamas. It starts with intention, deciding what matters most to you and living it out, one moment at a time.

Try This: Define Your Family Values

Ask yourself:

- *What feelings do I want my home to embody? (Love, safety, fun, respect, curiosity, adventure?)*
- *What are 3 values I want my children and stepchildren to inherit?*
- *What daily actions support those values?*

For example:

- If kindness is a core family value, how do you model that in daily life?
- If adventure is something you value, how do you create that in your home?
- If honest communication is a pillar, how do you ensure your home is a safe space where feelings are respected?

The key is intentionality—choosing what matters and making sure your actions reflect it.

If connection is a core value, maybe that looks like device-free dinners.

If resilience matters, maybe it's about praising effort over perfection.

If creativity is key, maybe it's dance parties in the kitchen or leaving time for unstructured play.

Reflection: Healing and Rewriting Your Story

Take a few quiet minutes to reflect:

- What messages did I receive about family growing up?
- What parts of my upbringing do I want to pass on?
- What parts do I want to consciously rewrite?

Journal Prompt: Write a letter to your younger self.

Tell her about the kind of family you are creating now. The safety you're building. The love that grows slowly but deeply. Remind her she didn't have to have it all figured out to be a good mom or stepmom, just willing.

At the end of the day, a strong, connected family isn't built by blood alone.

It's built by the choices we make every day to love, to communicate, to show up, even when it's hard.

Your past doesn't define the family you create; you do.

In every family—blended, biological, chosen, or something in between—there's an anchor. Someone who chooses presence over perfection. Grace over control. Intention over old patterns.

Let that be you.

Your story doesn't have to repeat own upbringing.
Your family doesn't have to look like anyone else's.
You get to build something new, something beautiful, healing, and whole.
Let your lagoon be a space of belonging.
Let your presence be the soft ground your family returns to.

Whether you are raising biological children, stepchildren, or a beautifully blended mix of both, know this: What matters most is the love, stability, and presence you bring. Because in the end, love isn't about getting it perfect; it's about showing up and holding steady through every tide. So, let's build something beautiful.

As I reflected on what it means to be a steady force for my kids, I realized something profound: parenting, no matter the shape it takes, isn't about controlling the outcome. It's about planting seeds. It's about showing up, staying grounded, and modeling the kind of resilience, grace, and self-trust we hope to nurture in our children.

And that leads us to the next chapter.

Because whether we're raising toddlers, teenagers, or supporting adult children on their own paths, our role isn't to clear the waves for them; it's to teach them how to ride them. To raise kids who are confident, compassionate, and equipped to navigate life's tides with courage.

Let's explore what it really takes to raise empowered, emotionally grounded kids in today's world and how we can become the lighthouse they return to when the seas get rough.

Chapter 8

Raising Confident, Empowered Kids: Giving Them the Tools to Navigate Life's Waves

If there's one thing I've learned about motherhood, it's that we can't protect our kids from every storm.

I've tried, believe me. I've sat through quiet car rides after heartbreaks, listened to the pain behind their words, and offered all the comfort I could muster even when I knew I couldn't fix things. I've watched my stepsons navigate first relationships and first breakups, aching to take the hurt away, to say the perfect thing that would make it all better. I've walked the line between giving space and showing up, wanting so badly for them to feel seen, supported, and understood.

And while every instinct in me wants to shield them from pain, I've come to realize that what they need most isn't protection—it's preparation. They need to know how to move through hard things, not avoid them. They need to believe they're strong enough to handle whatever comes.

As much as we'd love to create a life for them that is smooth sailing, where they never experience disappointment, failure, or heartache, the reality is that we can't control the waves they'll face.

What we can do is teach them how to navigate those waves with confidence.

We can't promise them an easy journey, but we can give them the tools to steer their own ship.

And that's what this chapter is all about: raising kids who are strong, adaptable, and secure in who they are so that no matter what life throws at them, they'll know how to keep moving forward.

When I think about what I want most for my children, it's not that they ace every test or win every award. It's that they:

- Know who they are.
- Feel secure expressing their needs and emotions.
- Believe they can face challenges and figure things out.
- Understand that failure isn't a verdict; it's part of the process.
- Trust themselves, even when life gets messy.

Empowerment isn't about shielding them from struggle. It's about walking alongside them, teaching them that they're capable—even when things are hard.

So how do we raise kids who are connected, courageous, and confident?

In the last chapter, we explored what it means to build a strong, connected family and how that work often starts with looking inward. We talked about how motherhood has a way of bringing our own childhood experiences to the surface, sometimes unexpectedly. I shared how becoming a mom made me reflect on the family I came from, the patterns I inherited, and the kind of legacy I want to leave behind.

This chapter builds on that foundation.

Because here's the truth: If we want to raise emotionally secure, empowered kids, we have to begin by doing the work ourselves.

I always thought parenting was about teaching. But what I didn't expect was how often I'd be the student, learning to recognize my triggers, unlearn old habits, and show up differently than what was modeled for me.

This healing work isn't always comfortable, but it's essential. Because every time we choose to respond with presence instead of reactivity, we're breaking a cycle. We're rewriting the story. And that work? It's the heart of raising empowered kids.

Psychologist Dr. Becky Kennedy (known as "Dr. Becky at Good Inside") reminds us: "Your child doesn't need a perfect parent. They need a connected one."

When we heal, we don't just change *our* lives. We change our children's lives too.

So before we dive into the tools and tactics, take a moment to honor how far you've come. You're not just showing up for your kids. You're showing up for the child you once were. And that's where true transformation begins.

Doing that inner work, unpacking our past, noticing our patterns, and choosing a new way forward isn't just healing for us. It creates a ripple effect that transforms how we show up as parents. When we begin to parent from a place of awareness instead of on autopilot, we make space for something powerful: intentionality. And that's where the shift happens.

Because once we've started doing that work within ourselves, we can begin to actively nurture the traits we hope to see in our kids. We can be more present in the hard moments, more attuned to their emotional needs, and more mindful in how we support their growth.

So now that we've laid the emotional foundation, let's talk about the practical ways we can raise kids who are not just surviving but thriving. Kids who trust themselves, express their emotions, and believe they can navigate whatever waves come their way.

Before we get into the tools, let me be clear: my kids are not perfect. And neither am I.

We've had biting phases, and we've had hitting phases (usually out of frustration but sometimes out of nowhere). There are days when getting out the door feels like a full-contact sport, and the only thing anyone is cooperating with is total chaos.

They're not the kids who always sit quietly in a circle or win the sportsmanship award at soccer. They're not trying out for team captain or giving motivational speeches to their classmates. But they are curious. Sensitive. Funny. Intelligent. And above all, they are perfectly themselves.

And that? That's more than enough.

So as you read through this next part, please don't see it as a formula for perfection. This isn't about raising "ideal" kids who never misbehave. This is about raising kids who feel safe in their skin. Kids who know their voice matters. Kids who can feel big feelings and still find their way through. Kids who trust themselves, even if the world hasn't always given them a reason to.

The tools I'm sharing here aren't quick fixes or one-size-fits-all strategies. They're small, intentional ways we can build our children's confidence and resilience over time.

Because confident, capable kids don't just appear out of thin air. They're nurtured, one messy, beautiful, grace-filled moment at a time.

1. Let Them Struggle (Even When It's Hard to Watch)

I'll admit, this one goes against every instinct I have as a mother.

Right now, the younger of my twins has started walking. He's wobbly but determined, toddling all over the place with growing confidence. But his older brother? He's not quite there yet. He watches, he tries, and sometimes he gets frustrated and gives up. And it's so hard to witness.

Every part of me wants to step in, to help him stand, to hold his hands, to somehow speed up the process so he doesn't feel left behind. But I know deep down that's not how he's going to learn. His journey will look different. And as much as I want to make things easier, my real job is to hold space for his frustration, his pace, and his process.

That's what raising empowered kids looks like. Not solving the struggle for them but walking alongside them as they figure things out on their own. Not rushing their growth but trusting it.

Confidence doesn't come from never facing hard things; it comes from learning we can handle them. When we jump in too quickly, we rob our kids of the chance to figure things out for themselves. And those moments? That's where real self-trust is born.

According to research from the Center on the Developing Child at Harvard University (2020), children who face age-appropriate challenges with adult support develop stronger problem-solving abilities, greater emotional regulation, and a deeper sense of agency.[17]

It doesn't mean we abandon them. It means we coach instead of rescue.

For older kids, try shifting your language:

- Instead of "Let me do that for you," try, "I know this is tricky. Want to try again together?"
- Instead of rushing in when they're frustrated, say, "I see that you're stuck. What do you think might help?"

Yes, it takes longer. Yes, it's messier. Yes, sometimes it ends in tears (from them or from you), but over time, those little moments of trying, failing, adjusting, and trying again are where resilience is built.

I've watched it happen in my own home.

Letting them struggle doesn't mean you're failing them. It means you're trusting them. And that trust? It's one of the greatest gifts we can give.

2. Teach Emotional Intelligence (Not Just "Toughness")

There's this outdated narrative, especially when raising boys, that "toughness" means not crying, not reacting, not feeling too deeply. That real strength is stoic and silent.

But I've learned (and am still learning) that true strength looks a lot different.

---

17 Center on the Developing Child at Harvard University. (2020). ***Building core capabilities for life: The science behind the skills adults need to succeed in parenting and in the workplace***. Harvard University. https://developingchild.harvard.edu/resources/building-core-capabilities-for-life/

It looks like being able to say, "I'm really mad right now" without hurting someone else.

It looks like knowing when to take a break.

It looks like feeling disappointed and still showing up the next day.

In our house, we've had plenty of moments where emotions run high, and that has resulted in the throwing of toys, collapsing in tears, and slamming doors. At first, my reaction was to shut it down: "You're fine," and "Stop crying." Not because I didn't care but because that's how I was taught to cope. To push feelings aside. To power through.

But I realized I wasn't teaching them strength. I was teaching them to disconnect from themselves.

Now, we do things differently.

We name feelings out loud:

- *It sounds like you're feeling frustrated. Do you want to talk about it?*

We practice coping tools together:

- *When I feel overwhelmed, I take a deep breath. Want to try it with me?*

We validate their emotional experiences:

- *It's okay to be sad. That was really disappointing.*

It's not perfect. There are still tantrums, still slammed doors. But there's also connection. There's language for things that used to just come out as screams or silence. There's a softness in knowing we can feel without falling apart.

Teaching emotional intelligence doesn't mean our kids won't struggle. It means they'll know how to move through struggle with self-awareness and eventually, self-compassion. And that's the kind of strength that lasts a lifetime.

3. Encourage Independence (Even When It's Messy)

Letting kids do things for themselves is one of those parenting lessons that sounds great in theory until you're staring at the clock, trying to get everyone ready for the day, and you realize it would be *so much faster* if you just did it all yourself.

Whether it's watching one twin try to feed himself while the other is trying to brush his own teeth, these little everyday moments test your patience. But they matter. Because confidence doesn't come from being told they're capable. It comes from experiencing it.

And it doesn't stop with the littles.

With the older boys, it's about giving them space to manage their own schoolwork, guiding them through time management, offering reminders but resisting the urge to jump in and rescue them at the last minute. When a big project is due and they're just starting the night before, every part of me wants to fix it, to lay out the steps, or even just give them the answer. But I've learned that growth doesn't come from perfection—it comes from practice.

So whether it's spilled cereal, mismatched socks, or a rough draft done just in time, I remind myself: They're not just learning what to do. They're learning that they can do hard things. They can plan, problem-solve, and figure things out for themselves even when it's messy.

And yes, it's often loud. And slower than we'd like. But it's also laying the foundation for self-trust. Studies show that giving children opportunities to make choices and take initiative—even in small ways—contributes to stronger self-esteem, motivation, and executive function development.[18]

So much of parenting is about planting seeds we may not see bloom right away. Encouraging independence, holding space for frustration, and trusting the process is all part of raising confident, empowered kids. But just as we nurture their growth, it's important to reflect on our own.

---

18 Deci, E. L., & Ryan, R. M. (2000). The "what" and "why" of goal pursuits: Human needs and the self-determination of behavior. ***Psychological Inquiry, 11***(4), 227–268. https://doi.org/10.1207/S15327965PLI1104_01

The following Activities and Reflections are here to help you pause, reconnect with your intentions, and create meaningful, everyday moments that align with the kind of family culture you want to build. Let these exercises guide you not to perfection but to presence.

Activities & Reflections: Raising Empowered Kids

These exercises are designed to help you connect more deeply with your parenting style, reflect on your own growth, and create intentional moments with your children.

Reflection Activity: Waves from the Past

Purpose: Identify how your own upbringing may be influencing your parenting.

Prompt: What messages did I receive about emotions, struggle, and independence as a child?

- Were you allowed to express anger or sadness?
- Did adults in your life step in quickly to "fix" things or let you figure them out?
- How were mistakes or failures managed?

Now ask yourself: *Which of those patterns am I unintentionally repeating, and which ones am I ready to break?*

Write freely and without judgment. Awareness is the first step toward change.

Connection Activity: The Confidence Jar (DIY)

Purpose: Build your child's self-trust and help them recognize their own growth.

How-To:

1. Grab a jar (or box) and decorate it together.
2. Cut small slips of paper and keep them nearby.

3. Each time your child tries something new, does something brave, or overcomes a challenge, write it down and add it to the jar.

Examples:

- "Tried broccoli even though you didn't want to."
- "Said sorry to your brother without being asked."
- "Put your shoes on all by yourself!"

Why it works: This simple act reinforces effort over perfection and gives kids a tangible reminder of their progress when they're feeling discouraged.

Emotional Intelligence Practice: Feelings First

Purpose: Help your child name, process, and express emotions.

Try This:

- Create a "Feelings Chart" together with faces and words for different emotions (sad, mad, excited, nervous, etc.).
- Hang it on the fridge or in a shared space.
- Once a day, ask: "Which feeling did you feel the most today?"
- Follow up with: "What made you feel that way?" or "What helped you feel better?"

This not only builds your child's emotional vocabulary but also strengthens your emotional connection.

Journal Prompts:

Use these prompts to reflect on how you're growing alongside your child:

- *What's one moment this week when I saw my child show confidence or resilience?*

- *When was the last time I modeled emotional regulation in front of my kids? What did I learn from it?*
- *What's one area where I can step back and allow more independence, even if it's messy?*
- *How can I celebrate small wins in our family this week?*
- *What's one thing I wish someone had told me as a child that I want to tell my kids now?*

The Goal is Not Perfection—It's Growth

We're not raising kids to have perfect lives. We're raising them to be adaptable, kind, emotionally aware humans who can face life's challenges with courage and grace.

We're growing alongside them. And every moment of imperfection is an opportunity for connection, for learning, for healing.

So, let's not just protect them from the storm. Let's teach them how to dance in the rain.

And as we nurture our kids, we can't forget the ecosystem that supports them, our relationships, especially our partnerships. Because raising confident kids becomes so much more sustainable when we're also building a strong, steady foundation with our partner.

Next up, we'll talk about how to strengthen that connection in the thick of parenthood and how to stay anchored in love, even when life feels like high tide.

Chapter 9

Strengthening Relationships: Building a Solid Partnership While Raising a Family

Motherhood changes everything, including your relationship.

The love that once felt effortless now has to compete with exhaustion, logistics, and a never-ending to-do list. Conversations that once revolved around dreams, vacations, or the next Netflix series now center on diaper duty, pickup schedules, and whether anyone remembered to switch the laundry.

Sometimes, it feels like you and your partner are ships passing in the night, dividing and conquering, surviving, but not really connecting.

I've been there.

I've vented to friends about the overwhelm, the imbalance, and yes, even the dishes. (And I've been honest with my husband about those frustrations too.) I've had moments where I felt like I was pouring everything into everything—my kids, my career, my creative projects—and had nothing left to give my relationship.

And yet, there are these grounding moments. Like the time the twins were both sick and couldn't go to daycare. Andrew and I spent the day tag-teaming the chaos. Tylenol, bottles, snuggles, and a lot of "Who's turn is it now?" It wasn't glamorous, but it reminded me: We're in this together.

These seasons test you, but they also deepen you.

Because a thriving family isn't just about raising happy, healthy kids. It's about nurturing the foundation that holds it all together—your partnership. When your relationship is strong, it creates stability, love, and security that ripples outward to your children, your home, and even your own sense of self.

So how do we keep our relationships strong in the chaos of parenting? How do we stay connected when life is pulling us in a million directions?

That's exactly what we're diving into in this chapter.

Before kids, relationships often feel like an open sea full of adventure, passion, and endless possibilities. You're both captains, steering the ship together, moving toward a shared future.

Then, kids come along, and suddenly, the waters change.
Suddenly, your ship is now filled with tiny, loud passengers who demand constant attention.

Someone always needs something, the sails are tattered, and sleep is a distant memory. At times, it may feel like you're steering in different directions.

But parenthood isn't supposed to replace your relationship. It's meant to evolve it. When you choose to navigate these new tides together, you don't just survive, you grow stronger, more connected, and more resilient.

The key is learning how to navigate this new season together instead of letting it pull you apart.

A relationship that survives and thrives through parenting isn't about never fighting, always agreeing, or constantly being in sync. It's about:

- Communication: Speaking honestly about what you need and how you feel
- Partnership: Seeing each other as teammates, not adversaries

- Respect: Valuing each other's visible and invisible contributions
- Connection: Intentionally making space for each other

And most of all?

It's about choosing each other over and over, especially when it's hard.

Laying that foundation of communication, respect, connection, and teamwork is essential. But knowing *what* makes a relationship strong is just the beginning.

The real work? It happens in the day-to-day.

It happens in how we speak to each other when we're running on fumes. In how we split the bedtime routine without keeping score. In whether we choose to stay connected when everything around us is pulling us in opposite directions.

And while there's no one-size-fits-all formula, there are a few tools that have helped Andrew and me stay grounded, even when life feels chaotic.

So let's break it down—real strategies, small shifts, and everyday practices that can help keep your relationship steady in the storm.

Tools for Strengthening Your Partnership While Raising a Family

1. Communication: More Than Just Logistics

One of the biggest relationship traps after kids is that most of your conversations become about logistics:

"Did you pack the lunches?"
"Can you pick up the kids from practice?"
"Did you pay the daycare bill?"

Let me be the first to say, this is something we're still figuring out.

Andrew and I don't have a perfectly polished communication style. We've had our fair share of misunderstandings, missed cues, and moments where one of us is talking and the other is mentally checking off the grocery list. We still fall into the trap of only talking about logistics or tag-teaming the kids without actually connecting with each other.

But here's the difference now: We're aware of it.

We're aware when we slip into "roommate mode." We recognize when we're operating more like coworkers than partners. And while we're far from perfect at fixing it in the moment, we've learned to circle back. To try again. To name what's missing and make a conscious effort to do better.

Because the truth is, knowing what makes communication stronger doesn't mean you'll nail it every time. But being intentional about it, choosing to notice, reflect, and reconnect when needed—that's where the growth happens.

So if you feel like most of your conversations revolve around school forms, pediatrician appointments, and "Did you thaw the chicken?" please know that you're not alone.

Let's talk about how we can shift those conversations from just surviving the day to actually seeing and supporting each other in it.

1. The 10-Minute Check-In

Every night (or as often as life allows) set aside just 10 minutes to connect. No kids, no to-do list, and *no screens.*

That last one might be the hardest. Because let's be honest, our phones are often the first thing we reach for when we finally have a moment of quiet. But being physically in the room isn't the same as being emotionally present, and your partner (like your kids) can feel the difference.

The famous *Still Face Experiment* conducted by Dr. Edward Tronick[19] shows that even very young children experience distress, confusion, and

---

19 Tronick, E. Z., Als, H., Adamson, L., Wise, S., & Brazelton, T. B. (1978). The infant's response to entrapment between contradictory messages in face-to-face interaction. *Journal of the American Academy of Child Psychiatry, 17*(1), 1–13. https://doi.org/10.1016/S0002-7138(09)62273-1

disconnection when a caregiver's face is unresponsive for just two minutes. Now imagine how that plays out when adults are mentally elsewhere or consistently emotionally unavailable and distracted by screens.

And it's not just kids. When we're distracted during our brief windows of togetherness, our partners begin to feel unseen too. Resentment builds not just from lack of help but from lack of presence.

So, during this check-in, create a phone-free zone. Set the timer if you have to. Sit next to each other on the couch or lie in bed and ask:

- "How are you *really* doing?"
- "What was the best part of your day?"
- "Is there anything you need more of from me right now?"

Resist the urge to fix. Just listen. Be there.

It sounds simple, and it is, but that doesn't make it easy. It's a practice. And over time, it can rekindle emotional connection in powerful ways, especially when everything else in your world is moving a mile a minute.

2. Playing on the Same Team: The Power of Partnership

Nothing builds resentment faster than feeling like you're carrying the mental or physical load alone.

One weekend, I found myself snapping about the dishes (again). Andrew didn't know I was keeping score in my head, but I was. Once I finally said it out loud, "I need you to just do the dishes without me asking!" he responded with, "Okay. I didn't realize it was piling up like that." That small moment of honesty shifted everything.

Try This: "I See You" Exercise

Once a week, tell your partner one specific thing you appreciate:

- "Thank you for cleaning up dinner. I know we were both exhausted."

- "I saw how patient you were with the kids today. That meant a lot."

Feeling seen matters. It fuels connection in quiet, powerful ways.

3. Keeping Intimacy Alive (Yes, Even When You're Tired)

Let's talk about the spark.

After kids, intimacy can feel like one more thing on the list. You're overstimulated, sleep-deprived, and emotionally maxed. But intimacy isn't just about sex. It's about closeness. It's the little gestures: a flirty glance, a hand on the back, an inside joke.

Try This: The "Small Sparks" Challenge

- Daily: One small act of affection. This could be a text, hug, or quick cuddle.
- Weekly: Create one shared moment, like a morning coffee, a walk, or watching a show together (even if it's *Dawson's Creek* reruns and debating the theme-song change!).
- Monthly: Schedule a date night (date nights at home count). One of our favorite things to do is stream the Key West sunset cam, kick back with boat drinks, and soak in that golden-hour magic right from our living room. It's our little slice of paradise, no babysitter required. Bonus points if there's a Jimmy Buffett song playing in the background. It's our way of channeling island time, even on the most chaotic days.

It is also important to learn your partner's love language. Andrew and I realized we express and receive love differently. Mine has shifted over the years from words of affirmation and quality time to acts of service, while his is physical touch. Knowing that helps us show up for each other more intentionally.

4. Navigating Conflict: Fighting Fair and Repairing Quickly

Conflict is inevitable, but it doesn't have to be damaging.

When we snap at each other, we try to "repair" quickly. That might look like a hug, a "Hey, I'm sorry I was short," or even a funny meme later in the day. Little repair rituals go a long way in maintaining trust.

Try This: "Pause and Reflect"

Before reacting, take a breath and ask:

- "Is this about *this* moment or something deeper (stress, exhaustion, feeling unappreciated)?"
- Choose curiosity over defensiveness.
- Then circle back. It doesn't have to be a full therapy session (which I do recommend doing separate from this), but acknowledging tension and reconnecting helps prevent resentment.

Reflect & Reconnect:
Journal Prompts for Strengthening Your Partnership

Use these prompts as a tool to reflect on your relationship in this season of life. There's no pressure to have all the answers. This is simply an invitation to notice, explore, and reconnect with intention.

Communication & Presence

- When was the last time we had a conversation that wasn't about the kids, work, or logistics? What did we talk about?
- In what ways do screens (phones, TV, etc.) impact our connection? Where could I be more intentional about presence?

- What is one thing I've been wanting to say but haven't found the words or time for?

Partnership and Support

- What's one specific thing my partner does that makes me feel supported or seen?
- What's one responsibility or task that's felt uneven lately? How can I communicate that with compassion and clarity?
- How do we currently divide parenting and household tasks? Is there something I'd like to revisit or adjust?

Intimacy and Connection

- What makes me feel close to my partner emotionally, physically, or mentally?
- What small daily or weekly rituals help us stay connected? Which ones do I want to bring back or strengthen?
- What's one loving or flirty gesture I can try this week to bring a little spark into our day?

Alignment and Growth

- What shared values anchor our relationship, even when life feels chaotic?
- What has our relationship taught me about myself since becoming a parent?
- How can we support each other's personal growth while still growing together?

At the end of the day, relationships don't thrive on grand gestures. They thrive on small, daily choices.

- The choice to listen.
- The choice to be present.
- The choice to appreciate instead of criticize.
- The choice to make time for each other, even in the chaos.

So, as you navigate the waves of parenthood, remember: You and your partner are on the same team.

And when you take the time to strengthen your foundation, it creates a ripple effect, one that makes your whole family stronger. Your kids feel more secure. Your home feels more connected. And *you* feel less like you're carrying it all alone.

But here's the thing: even the strongest partnership can't meet every need.

As much as we love and lean on our partners, we're still human. We still need outside support in the form of friendships that refill our cup, people we can vent to, laugh with, cry to. People who remind us who we are beyond the roles we play.

Because no matter how solid your relationship is, raising a family isn't meant to be done in isolation.

In the next chapter, we're going to explore how to build a support system that truly supports you—one that lifts you up, fills in the gaps, and reminds you that you don't have to do it all alone.

Chapter 10

You Don't Have to Do It Alone: Building the Support System Every Mother Deserves

We aren't meant to do this alone.

Motherhood, marriage, careers, life, it's all too much for one person to carry solo. And yet, so many of us try.

We wear our independence like a badge of honor. We convince ourselves that if we just work harder, plan better, push through the exhaustion, we can handle it all on our own.

But let's be real: Going it alone isn't sustainable.

We need people. We need support. We need community.

And yet, asking for help? That's one of the hardest things for so many of us to do.

I used to think that leaning on others meant I was failing in some way, like if I were truly strong, I'd be able to handle everything myself. But motherhood (and stepmotherhood) humbled me. It showed me that strength isn't about doing it all alone. Instead, it's about knowing when to ask for help.

Because the truth is, having a solid support system doesn't just make life easier; it makes life richer, more joyful, and more connected.

This chapter is all about finding your people, learning to ask without guilt for help, and building a support system that lifts you up instead of draining you.

Let's start with the hard part: Why is asking for help so damn difficult? For many women, it bumps up against a lifetime of beliefs about what it means to be "strong," "capable," or "a good mom."

You might recognize some of these thoughts:

- "I don't want to be a burden."
- "Everyone else seems to be handling it fine."
- "If I ask for help, I'll look weak."
- "It's just easier if I do it myself."

These beliefs don't appear out of nowhere. Many of us watched our mothers, grandmothers, and women around us do everything with little to no help and carry the load in silence. We internalized the idea that this is what "being strong" looks like.

But let's reframe it:

- Asking for help isn't weakness; it's wisdom.
- Letting people support you isn't a burden; it's a gift to them and to you.
- No one is "doing it all" on their own. We just don't see their behind-the-scenes.

And the biggest truth? You don't have to prove your worth by burning yourself out.

In previous generations, support systems were built into the fabric of daily life. Families lived close. Neighbors watched each other's kids. Grandparents, cousins, and aunties filled in the gaps.

Today? Many moms live far from family, don't know their neighbors, and feel pressure to appear as though they have it all together, especially in the filtered world of social media.

In fact, a 2022 study by Cigna found that 58% of mothers in the U.S. report feeling lonely on a regular basis, despite being surrounded by people.[20]

And the National Academy of Sciences confirms that loneliness and lack of social connection are as damaging to our health as smoking 15 cigarettes a day.[21]

We were never meant to mother in isolation. We were built for connection.

So yes, community matters. Deeply.

Not just for our mental health, or to ease the daily overwhelm (though it does both). But because it reminds us that we're human. That we belong. That we were never meant to carry everything on our own.

And yet, when we talk about "support," it can feel vague or unattainable, like something reserved for moms with built-in villages or extra resources. But the truth is, support doesn't have to be big or formal or perfectly curated. It just has to be *real.*

It starts with a few trusted people. The ones who see you. The ones who show up. The ones who help you hold it all—emotionally, practically, or even just energetically. And these are not just the people who are there when times are easy but people who:

- You can be your unfiltered self around.
- Show up when you need them (without keeping score).
- Remind you of who you are when you feel lost.
- Pour into you instead of only taking from you.

---

20 Cigna. (2022). ***Loneliness and the workplace: 2022 U.S. report***. Cigna Corporation. https://www.cigna.com/about-us/newsroom/studies-and-reports/loneliness-epidemic

21 Holt-Lunstad, J., Smith, T. B., Baker, M., Harris, T., & Stephenson, D. (2015). Loneliness and social isolation as risk factors for mortality: A meta-analytic review. ***Perspectives on Psychological Science, 10***(2), 227–237. https://doi.org/10.1177/1745691614568352

So, who are your go-to people?

To help you reflect, it can be helpful to think beyond just names and consider the roles different people play in your life. Support comes in many forms, and often, we need different types of connection for different moments.

Here are five types of support that every mom deserves in her circle. You might find all five in one or two people, or you might see these roles spread across your broader community. The key is recognizing them and nurturing those connections intentionally.

1. The No-Judgment Friend: The one who lets you vent, ugly cry, or show up exhausted without pretending to have it all together.
2. The Encourager: The one who reminds you of your strength when you doubt yourself.
3. The Problem-Solver: The one who helps you think through challenges and offers real solutions.
4. The Lighthearted One: The friend who makes you laugh, reminds you not to take life too seriously, and pulls you out of your funks.
5. The Helper: The person who shows up in tangible ways, bringing you coffee, watching your kids, or just making life feel a little easier.

Your circle might look different, and that's okay. The goal is not perfection. It's connection.

And sometimes, it's in the smallest, most ordinary moments that you realize just how much that support means.

I still remember the first time I tried to take the babies and the dog out for a walk by myself. It felt like preparing for a cross-country trek, diaper bag packed, bottles ready, dog leash in hand, and the double stroller that somehow always felt like wrangling a small parade float.

But I wasn't alone. My friend came with me that day—not to push the stroller, not to walk the dog, but simply to be there. She knew what a big deal it was. We didn't talk about it like it was monumental, but her presence reminded me I didn't have to brave that new chapter without backup.

That walk was chaotic and beautiful. The dog zigzagged, the babies fussed, and I probably looked like a hot mess to anyone driving by. But I did it. And I did it because I wasn't trying to prove I could do it all alone; I had someone walking beside me.

That's what support looks like. It's not always about solving the hard stuff. It's about sitting with you in it. It's about the friends who show up for the everyday moments that feel big when you're in them.

And once we've experienced that kind of care, it becomes easier to recognize just how much we need it and how to ask for it.

How to Ask for Help (Without Feeling Guilty)

All right, so you know you *need* support. But how do you actually ask for it without guilt or awkwardness?

Step 1: Identify Where You Need Help

Think about your biggest pain points right now. What's draining your energy the most? Where are you feeling unsupported?

Here are some common areas:

- Parenting (childcare, school pick-ups, extra hands on hard days).
- Emotional support (someone to listen, encourage, check in).
- Household tasks (meal help, rides, housework).
- Career balance (networking, flexible schedules, mentorship).

Once you know where you need help, it's easier to ask for something specific.

Step 2: Use the Right Language

So often, we overcomplicate asking for help because we feel like we need to justify it or apologize for it. When the twins were born, I learned the hard way that vague cries for help don't work. But what *does* work?

- Be direct: Instead of *"I hate to ask, but..."* say *"Could you watch the boys while I take the dog for a walk? Would you be open to that?"*
- Be clear: People want to help, but they don't always know how. Instead of *"I'm overwhelmed,"* say *"Could you pick up the kids one day this week?"*
- Receive with gratitude, not guilt: Instead of *"I feel bad asking,"* say *"Thank you, this really helps me out."*

Step 3: Accept Help When It's Offered

How many times has someone said, *"Let me know if you need anything,"* and you responded with *"Oh, I'm fine!"* even when you weren't?

Next time, take them up on it.

- If a friend offers to bring a meal? Say yes.
- If a coworker offers to share the workload? Accept it.
- If your partner says, *"Go take a break; I've got this,"* believe them.

Letting people help isn't a weakness. It's a strength.

Learning how to ask for help is a powerful first step. It opens the door to connection, honesty, and a more sustainable rhythm of life. But asking is just part of the equation.

Support isn't only about what we receive. It's also about what we create.

Once we begin to shift our mindset about asking for and accepting help, we can take it a step further: actively building a village—not just for emergencies or busy seasons but for daily life. A community that lifts you up, celebrates with you, and walks beside you through the beautiful, the boring, and the barely-holding-it-together moments.

Let's talk about how to build that kind of village even if it feels like you're starting from scratch.

Building a Village (Even If You Feel Like You Don't Have One)

You don't need 20 people. You just need *your* people.

Here's how to begin:

1. Start With What You Have

Look around as your village may already be forming:

- A coworker who checks in on you.
- A fellow parent from the soccer sidelines.
- Someone from your running group.

Nurture those connections. Start small. Be consistent.

2. Put Yourself in Community Spaces

It's hard to make new friends as an adult. It's awkward. But it's worth it.

Places to try:

- Local parenting meetups or classes.
- Faith-based communities.
- Kids' activities and school events.

- Fitness groups or clubs. (I'm forever grateful to my Turtle running group—your encouragement, laughs, and early morning miles have meant more than you know.)
- Online mom groups that meet IRL.

Not sure what to say? Try:

- "I'm new here. How long have you been coming?"
- "This might sound random, but would you want to grab coffee sometime?"
- "I'm trying to make more mom friends, and it's surprisingly hard."

The conversation doesn't have to be perfect. It just has to be *real.*

3. Be the One Who Reaches Out

If you're feeling lonely, chances are someone else is too.

Start the group text. Plan the walk. Host the low-pressure playdate with paper plates and no judgment.

The more we normalize *showing up,* the easier it becomes for everyone.

4. Create a Culture of Support

- Let go of surface-level friendships and choose depth.
- Be honest when someone asks how you're doing.
- Offer help and accept it.
- Celebrate your friends. Check in on them. Share the load.

When you create that energy, it comes back to you.

Here's the most beautiful part about creating a strong support system: It doesn't just help you; it helps everyone around you.

When we allow ourselves to be supported:

- We show our kids that asking for help is normal and healthy.
- We break the cycle of over-functioning and silent suffering.
- We create space for deeper, more meaningful relationships.

And, perhaps most importantly, we remind ourselves that we are not meant to do this alone.

Building a village doesn't happen overnight. It's something we cultivate over time—one conversation, one shared moment, one brave invitation at a time. And like anything meaningful, it starts with intention.

So before you move on, let's pause.

Let's take a breath, look around, and get honest about where support is already showing up in your life and where there's room to invite more in.

These next few prompts are here to help you reflect, take action, and begin building the kind of support system that truly sustains you.

Exercises for Reflection and Action

Exercise 1: Mapping Your Support System

- List 5 people in your life who support you emotionally, physically, or mentally.
- Identify one area where you could use more help.
- Commit to asking one person for support this week.

Exercise 2: Creating Your "Help List"

- Write down 5 specific tasks that would make your life easier (e.g., help with school pick-ups, someone to vent to, meal support).
- Next time someone asks, *"Let me know if you need anything,"* refer to your list and ask for something tangible.

Exercise 3: The Community Ripple Effect

Think about one way you can contribute to your village.

Could you:

- Start a text thread for local moms?
- Offer to help a friend?
- Be the one who invites others in?

Small actions create big ripples. What's one step you can take this month?

We Rise Together

Motherhood isn't meant to be done in isolation. And yet, so many of us struggle in silence, believing we have to be everything to everyone.

But real strength? It's knowing that we're better together.

So, Mermaid Mama, let yourself be supported. Find your people. Ask for help. Let go of guilt.

Because when you do, you don't just lighten your own load. You create ripples of connection, community, and love that extend far beyond yourself.

Of course, finding support isn't just about survival. It's also about sustainability.

When you're raising a family *and* building a career, the stakes are higher, the pressure is greater, and the need for support becomes even more critical.

So in the next chapter, we'll explore what it means to pursue your purpose while raising your people, and we'll look at how to do it in a way that honors both your ambition and your motherhood.

Because you don't have to choose one or the other.

You were made to rise in both.

Chapter 11

Navigating Career and Motherhood: Redefining Success on Your Terms

You've started building your village. You're learning to ask for help. You're letting go of the lie that you have to do it all alone.

And now comes the next layer of the dance, the part where you're not just raising your family but also raising your hand. For the meeting. For the opportunity. For the dream you still want to chase.

Because here's the truth: You are not *just* a mother. You're a woman with ambition, creativity, and a fire inside you that still matters. And yet, pursuing those things while caring for tiny humans can feel like juggling water. The pressure is real. That's why this chapter is about reclaiming your ambition, rewriting the rules, and designing a career that allows you to thrive as both a mother and a professional.

According to the U.S. Bureau of Labor Statistics, nearly 72% of mothers with children under 18 are part of the workforce,[22] and a Pew Research report indicates that 54% of working mothers felt they couldn't give 100% at work due to balancing work and parenting responsibilities, compared to 43% of working fathers.[23]

---

22 U.S. Bureau of Labor Statistics. (2023). ***Employment characteristics of families—2022*** (Report USDL-23-0714). https://www.bls.gov/news.release/pdf/famee.pdf

23 Pew Research Center. (2022, May 6). ***Working moms in the U.S. have faced challenges on multiple fronts during the pandemic***. https://www.pewresearch.org/short-reads/2022/05/06/working-moms-in-the-u-s-have-faced-challenges-on-multiple-fronts-during-the-pandemic/

These numbers don't just reflect data; they reflect our daily lives. The mental load, the schedule juggling, the constant push to "do it all" can leave even the most capable women feeling stretched thin.

But here's the truth we don't hear often enough:

- You can have a career you love and a fulfilling family life.
- You can be ambitious and be a present, loving mother.
- You can chase your dreams while also prioritizing your home and relationships.

But you can't do it all, all at once, at full capacity, all the time.

It isn't about splitting yourself evenly between work and family every single day. It's about being fully present in the role that needs you most at any given moment, without guilt.

Some seasons will require more focus on your career.

Some seasons will require you to pull back.

Some days, you'll be a rock star at work.

Some days, you'll be an absolute mess, just trying to get everyone fed.

And all of it is okay.

The key is learning how to shift with the tides instead of fighting against them.

I've lived that tension. The guilt of stepping away from work when one of the twins had a fever. The overwhelm of pumping while driving to client meetings across the state. The tug-of-war between showing up for my family and showing up for my goals.

What I learned is that you *can* be devoted and driven. You *can* build a meaningful career and be a present, loving mother. You *can* thrive in both—just not at full throttle all the time. The secret is redefining what success looks like *now.*

So what does success look like when you're not trying to be everything to everyone? It starts with redefining it on your own terms.

For so long, we've been fed a version of success that measures worth in productivity, titles, or perfectly curated moments. But motherhood has a way of flipping all of that upside down. Suddenly, success isn't about climbing the ladder; it's about being grounded in your values. It's not about having it all; it's about honoring what matters most in *this* season.

When I was on maternity leave after having my twins, I was determined to keep up the same pace. I thought I could be extra efficient, with detailed schedules, app-based calendars, and time-blocked days. I told myself, *I've got this.*

And then reality hit.

Between sleepless nights, feedings, and the mental load of new motherhood, I was drowning. No planner or productivity hack could fix the fact that I was trying to live like I hadn't just birthed two babies.

Eventually, I gave myself permission to shift. To rest. To re-prioritize. I started riding the waves instead of trying to outrun them.

The truth is, you are allowed to evolve your definition of success as you evolve, and that's not failure—that's growth.

That mindset helped me make a bold but necessary decision: I decided to change jobs. Not because I didn't love my work but because I knew the career I had didn't support the life I was living. I needed flexibility, grace, and alignment. And I found a role that honored this season of life, one that allowed me to show up fully for my family and for myself.

Making that change was both terrifying and freeing. It felt like diving into uncharted waters, unsure of what I'd find but knowing I couldn't keep swimming against the current. And once I surfaced with a new role that truly supported my life, I started seeing something else more clearly, too.

It wasn't just about finding a better job. It was about shedding the outdated belief that I had to be everything to everyone, all the time.

That's when I began to see the real myth we've been sold, this idea that we're supposed to "have it all" in order to be successful.

For years, I measured success by productivity, promotions, and external validation.

But motherhood changed that. I started asking deeper questions:

- Does my work align with my values?
- Can I be present for my family and still feel creatively fulfilled?
- What am I willing to say no to so I can say yes to what matters most?

Success now looks like:

- Doing work that feels purposeful.
- Having the flexibility to be present.
- Protecting my mental and emotional health.
- Creating a life that feels sustainable.

Success is no longer defined by hustle. It's defined by harmony. Just like the ocean, your life isn't meant to be static. It moves in rhythms and waves. Some days, you lead with your ambition. Other days, you let the current of motherhood take the lead.

There is no one-size-fits-all answer to navigating career and motherhood. But what I've learned is that success doesn't have to look the way it did before.

It's not about choosing work or family. It's about creating a definition of success that aligns with who you are now, in this season of life.

Redefining success is the first step, an internal shift in how you see yourself, your worth, and what you're building. But once the inner tide turns, the questions become: How do you shape your outer world to match? How do you build a career that doesn't just float but flows with your life?

Let's explore the practical ways to anchor your ambitions while honoring the season you're in.

How to Build a Career That Works for Your Life

So, how do we actually navigate career and motherhood in a way that feels sustainable?

Here are some key strategies:

1. Identify Your Priorities in This Season

Instead of trying to do everything, focus on what matters most right now.

Try This: The "Season of Life" Reflection

- What do I need from my career in this season? (Stability, growth, flexibility, creativity?)
- What do I need from my personal life in this season? (More time with family, space to recharge, financial security?)
- What small adjustments can I make to align my career with these priorities?

Your priorities will shift, and that's okay. Give yourself permission to re-evaluate as you grow.

2. Set Boundaries That Protect Your Energy

Boundaries are essential if you want to avoid burnout.

- At work: Set clear work hours, say no to unnecessary commitments, and delegate when possible.
- At home: Communicate your needs to your partner, schedule non-negotiable personal time, and release the guilt around asking for help.

- For yourself: Learn to protect your mental space, stop checking emails late at night, unfollow accounts that make you feel like you're not doing enough, and prioritize rest.

Try This: Create a Boundary Script

- *"I don't check emails after 6 p.m."*
- *"I can't take on extra work right now, but I appreciate you thinking of me."*
- *"I need an hour to myself in the evenings to recharge."*

Boundaries aren't selfish. They're necessary for long-term success and happiness.

3. Build a Career That Aligns With Your Values

If your current career doesn't feel aligned with the life you want, it may be time to make a shift.

Ask yourself:

- *Does my job support my personal goals and family life?*
- *Am I passionate about what I do?*
- *Do I feel fulfilled, or am I just going through the motions?*

If something feels off, explore options like:

- Negotiating flexible work arrangements.
- Pivoting to a new role or industry.
- Starting a business or freelancing.
- Scaling back temporarily to focus on family.

Remember: Your career is a journey, not a fixed destination. It's okay to evolve and make changes as you grow.

You've redefined success. You've started making small shifts. You've protected your energy, realigned your career, and begun honoring your season.

But what happens when the tide changes again?

Because it will.

What you need isn't just strategy. You need something to return to when life gets chaotic again—a guide, a rhythm, a way to move with purpose.

That's where F.L.O.W. comes in.

In the ocean of motherhood and ambition, your power comes from learning to move with the tide, not against it. F.L.O.W. is a flexible, values-based rhythm that helps you navigate the shifting demands of life with clarity and grace.

F—Foundations (Your Core Values)

This is your anchor. The bedrock beneath the waves.

Ask yourself:

- What do I want my life to stand for?
- How do I want to show up for my family and career?
- Which 3–5 values are non-negotiable to me?

Try This: Write your top 5 values on sticky notes. Put them somewhere visible and use them to guide decisions big and small.

L—Legacy Goals (Your Ambition and Career Vision)

Legacy isn't about what you leave behind. It's about what you're building now.

Ask yourself:

- What impact do I want to make through my work?
- What does career fulfillment look like in this season?
- What's one step I can take toward that this month?

Try This: Write down 3 legacy goals (short- or long-term). Keep them next to your values and revisit them weekly.

O—Oasis Moments (Family and Personal Well-Being)

These are the sacred, soul-filling moments that refuel you.

Ask yourself:

- What small rituals bring me joy?
- Am I fully present in the moments that matter most?
- How can I protect those moments with intention?

Try This: Schedule one Oasis Moment this week that's just for you or your family and honor it like any other commitment.

W—Waves and Boundaries (Your Rhythm and Protection)

Life comes in waves. Boundaries help you ride them instead of being swept away by them.

Ask yourself:

- Where am I overextending?
- What rhythms help me feel grounded?
- What boundaries will protect my time and peace?

Try This: Draft one simple boundary script:

- "I'm not available for late meetings."
- "I need a quiet hour each morning to reset."

F.L.O.W. Mapping Exercise

Create your own F.L.O.W. Map:

F—Your top 3 values

L—One meaningful career goal

O—A ritual or moment that grounds you

W—One boundary you will honor this week

When things feel heavy or chaotic, return to this map. Let it guide you not toward perfection but back into harmony.

Understanding your F.L.O.W. is more than an exercise; it's a mindset shift. It gives you a grounded, graceful way to move through the waves of motherhood and career without losing yourself in the undertow.

Now, let's take that clarity and put it into motion.

The following reflection activities are here to help you anchor into what matters most, realign when things feel off, and chart a course that supports both your ambition and your heart.

Because the more you return to your flow, the more confident, centered, and powerful you become.

Reflection Exercises

- Write down your new definition of success. "What matters most to me in this season?"
- "What shifts do I need to make to align my career with my new definition?"

- "Where in my life do I feel most in flow, and where do I feel like I am fighting the current?"

At the end of the day, no one else gets to define what success looks like for you.

Not society.

Not your boss.

Not even your past self.

You get to decide.

So, Mermaid Mama, let go of the guilt. Release the pressure to "do it all." Trust that you are exactly where you need to be, and you are capable of creating a life that honors both your ambition and your heart.

The waves may shift, but you? You are strong enough to navigate them all.

Your career is *yours* to design.

It doesn't have to fit society's expectations.

It doesn't have to look like what it did before motherhood.

It doesn't have to be all or nothing.

You are allowed to evolve, shift, and create a work life that aligns with who you are now.

Because when you align your work with your values? That's where true success begins.

And now that you've redefined success on your terms, you've created space for both your career and your family. And you've anchored into your values and begun to flow with the rhythm of your life, not against it.

We've spent Part 2 diving deep into the heart of the lagoon—our families, our careers, our relationships, and the delicate balance of motherhood and ambition. We've explored what it means to build a strong, connected home, to navigate the push and pull of work and family, and to redefine success on our own terms.

But now, it's time to expand outward.

Because when we feel grounded in who we are and how we show up at home and at work, we begin to look outward with open hands and a full heart.

Part 3 is about that expansion. It's about how we take everything we've learned about motherhood, ambition, wellness, and self and use it to make waves beyond our own shorelines. Whether it's in our communities, our advocacy, our leadership, or the quiet, everyday ways we uplift others, this next part is about living our purpose out loud.

Let's dive into what it means to lead, serve, and shine in a way that honors both our hearts and the world around us.

Because as much as motherhood and career shape us, there's a world beyond our daily responsibilities, a world that needs our presence, our energy, and our impact.

As women, as mothers, as leaders, we are part of something bigger. We are part of communities, ecosystems, and movements that extend beyond the walls of our homes and offices. And when we connect with the world around us, when we root ourselves in something greater than our own schedules and to-do lists, we find a deeper sense of purpose, healing, and harmony.

So let's take everything we've built within ourselves and within our homes, and let's expand outward. Let's ride the currents of change, healing, and impact. Let's step into a bigger conversation, one that connects us to the planet, to future generations, and to the rhythms of life itself.

Part 3:

MAKING WAVES—CARRYING THE HEART OF MOTHERHOOD INTO THE WORLD

Motherhood doesn't end at the edge of our homes. It doesn't stop at the lunchboxes we pack, the tears we wipe, or the goals we chase.

Motherhood is expansive. It teaches us to care deeply, lead intuitively, love fiercely. And that energy doesn't just shape our children. It has the power to shape the world.

Once we've found a rhythm within ourselves and created a sense of flow in our families and careers, a natural question begins to arise: What now?

The answer? We expand.

We look beyond our own four walls and ask how we can use our voice, our values, and our gifts to create ripples of healing, hope, and change in the world around us. Whether it's nurturing our communities, protecting the planet, mentoring other women, or simply showing up with compassion, we begin to mother more than just our children.

We begin to mother the world.
We begin to mother with the world.

Mother Earth has always been our teacher. She shows us how to bloom in our seasons, how to weather storms with grace, and how to return to stillness when the world feels too loud. Her rhythms are our rhythms; her tides, our tides.

This part of the book is about that expansion.

It's about understanding that the small, intentional ways we show up matter. That nature isn't just a place to retreat; it's a source of wisdom and grounding that can guide how we lead and live. That community isn't just a support system; it's a shared space where our impact multiplies.

You don't have to change the whole world to make a difference.

But you do have the power to send ripples outward that reach farther than you may ever know.

Let's begin there, by honoring the quiet power of small actions and walking in step with Mother Earth as we create waves of lasting change.

Chapter 12

The Ripple Effect: How Small Actions Create Big Change in the World

The most powerful changes often don't start with grand gestures. They start with small, quiet moments that leave a lasting impression.

When I was young, my mom worked night shifts, and I remember how she would sometimes call in to the *Delilah* radio show to dedicate songs to me and my brother. We'd be home listening, and suddenly, through the static of the radio, we'd hear our names and a message from her, wrapped in a song. In those moments, I felt seen. Loved. Connected.

I didn't realize it at the time, but those nighttime dedications planted something deep inside me. I saw how the simple act of sharing a message through a voice on the airwaves could touch people, lift them up, and make them feel less alone. That's where my love for communication began. That was the spark.

Even as a child, I sensed that words carried power. That stories, when spoken with heart, could become lifelines. I've been chasing that sense of purpose ever since, and I feel so grateful to say I've found it.

Whether it's through coaching, mission-driven campaigns, or community initiatives, I now get to use my voice to create impact. And just like those late-night dedications, my goal is the same: to let people know they matter, that they're not alone, and that someone is cheering them on.

That's the magic of small actions. A message. A song. A gesture. A story. You never know who's listening or how far your ripple will travel.

There's a saying I love:

"Individually, we are one drop. Together, we are an ocean."

At times, the weight of the world can feel like too much to carry. Climate change. Injustice. Division. Pollution. The mental load of motherhood, career, and personal responsibilities is already heavy, so how do we possibly create impact beyond our own shores?

Here's the truth: You don't have to change the entire world to create change. You just have to start where you are.

Every small action, every choice, every conversation, every moment of kindness sends out a ripple.

And ripples? They expand.

Research in behavioral science shows that when one person adopts a positive behavior, it significantly increases the chances that their close network will do the same. This is called behavioral contagion—and it's proof that the smallest decisions can influence far beyond what we can see.[24]

Whether it's in our families, our communities, or the wider world, the way we live *does* matter. And when we show up in small, intentional ways again and again? Those ripples become waves.

This chapter is an invitation to embrace that truth: You are already a force for change.

When we see major global problems, environmental destruction, systemic inequality, suffering, it's tempting to think: *What can one person really do?*

But here's what's often overlooked: Every big movement began with small steps.

---

24 Fowler, J. H., & Christakis, N. A. (2008). ***Dynamic spread of happiness in a large social network: Longitudinal analysis over 20 years in the Framingham Heart Study***. BMJ, 337, a2338. https://doi.org/10.1136/bmj.a2338

Think about it:

- One person choosing to use a reusable water bottle can replace over 150 plastic bottles a year.
- A single act of kindness can alter someone's mental health, shift their day, or change their life.
- A child raised in a home that talks about empathy, justice, and sustainability carries those values into their future world.

According to the Ellen MacArthur Foundation, over 80% of ocean plastic pollution starts on land,[25] which means daily choices (like reducing single-use plastics) aren't just symbolic. They're direct action.

The world doesn't change because one person does everything.
It changes because many people do small, meaningful things, consistently, over time.

So where do we begin?

When everything feels urgent, it helps to zoom in.

Impact isn't always about sweeping gestures; it's about understanding the layers of influence you already carry.
That's where the ripple metaphor becomes so powerful.

Just like a drop of water sends out rings that expand outward, the way we live—how we speak, care, consume, and connect—ripples from our inner world to our community and eventually to the wider world.

Let's explore what that looks like, one circle at a time.

When we think about making an impact, it helps to break it down into 3 circles:

---

25 Ellen MacArthur Foundation. (2016). ***The new plastics economy: Rethinking the future of plastics***. https://ellenmacarthurfoundation.org/the-new-plastics-economy-rethinking-the-future-of-plastics

1. The Inner Ripple: *Ourselves and Our Home*
2. The Middle Ripple: *Our Community*
3. The Outer Ripple: *The Larger World*

Each layer builds upon the next, meaning that change always starts with us.

The Inner Ripple: Yourself and Your Home

This is where everything begins.

Before we can lead change outwardly, we must look inward.

Ask yourself:

- Am I living in alignment with what I care about?
- What messages am I modeling for my kids through my daily choices?

Try This:

- Swap single-use items for reusables: water bottles, grocery bags, lunch containers.
- Start conversations with your kids about empathy, inclusion, and environmental care.
- Support sustainable brands and reduce waste at home.

Even one child watching you compost, donate, or stand up for fairness is a ripple that will travel far beyond your reach.

The Middle Ripple: Community

Change expands when we step outside our door and into the places where we live, work, and gather.

You don't have to start a nonprofit to make a difference in your neighborhood, you just have to show up.

Over the years, I've had the honor of contributing to campaigns that embody the spirit of community-led change. One that holds a special place in my heart is the *No Horsin' Around* initiative in my Central Florida community, a creative and collaborative effort to inspire behavior change and reduce littering. This campaign was a powerful reminder that advocacy doesn't have to be loud or large-scale to be effective. Often, meaningful change begins with people who care deeply and take action in their own back yard.

Try This:

- Shop local: Support women-owned or eco-conscious businesses.
- Get involved: Volunteer, attend a town hall meeting, start a book club or community cleanup.
- Use your voice: Share values on social media or write letters to local leaders.

The Outer Ripple: The Larger World

You don't need a global platform to make a global impact.

What you do with your time, money, and attention matters.

Try This:

- Choose brands committed to ethical labor, clean ingredients, and sustainability.
- Make small but regular donations to causes you believe in.
- Sign petitions, vote mindfully, and stay informed without being overwhelmed.

Change doesn't require perfection. It requires momentum.

According to Giving USA, the majority of nonprofit support comes from individual donors, not corporations.[26] That $10 you give each month? It's part of a wave.

As you move through these layers of impact, from your home to your community to the world, you might feel both inspired and a little overwhelmed. That's normal.

Because with awareness often comes pressure: *Am I doing enough? Am I doing it right?*

But the truth is, you don't have to carry the weight of the world to make a meaningful difference.

Before we move on, let's talk about how to stay grounded and motivated—without burning out.

The biggest barrier to action isn't apathy; it's overwhelm.

So how do we keep showing up when the world feels heavy?

Reframe the Pressure:

- You're not meant to fix everything. Focus on what's *yours* to carry.
- Progress matters more than perfection.
- The ripple effect is real. You are part of something bigger than you know.

Ask Yourself:

- What lights me up?
- Where do I feel most called to act?
- What can I *realistically* commit to right now?

---

26 Giving USA Foundation. (2023). *Giving USA 2023: The annual report on philanthropy for the year 2022*. Lilly Family School of Philanthropy. https://givingusa.org

Start there. And return to it as often as you need.

A Note on Grace: This Season Might Not Be Your Most Impact-Driven, and That's Okay

If you're reading this while holding a baby on your hip or running on three hours of sleep, I want you to hear this clearly: You don't have to do it all right now.

This season of new motherhood has not been my most sustainable, eco-conscious, or outward facing. There have been weeks when the laundry piled up, where I forgot to recycle, where I grabbed convenience food wrapped in plastic because I was just trying to survive the day.

And you know what? That's okay.

We don't create change from guilt. We create it from love, awareness, and intention.

What matters most is that you care. That you're trying. That you're *aware*. Small steps taken from a place of compassion, especially compassion for yourself, are still steps in the right direction.

So give yourself permission to be where you are.

Let this chapter serve as a gentle reminder: The ripple effect starts with grace.
And sometimes, the most radical act of impact in a chaotic world is simply showing up with love—for your child, for your community, and yes, for yourself.

So often, we underestimate the power of our own presence, our choices, our words, our energy. But the truth is, every small, intentional step you take creates movement. You are already making ripples, just by caring. Just by trying. Just by being a conscious, compassionate mother navigating it all.

But reflection is what helps those ripples expand with clarity and purpose.

Before we close this chapter, let's take a moment to turn inward, to connect the dots between your values, your actions, and the impact you want to have on the world around you. The following activities and prompts are here to help you pause, reflect, and move forward with intention. Let's explore your ripple effect, one small wave at a time.

Reflection and Action: Embracing Your Ripple Effect

1. Values Alignment Check-In

Journal Prompts:

- *What are 3 core values I want to embody in my daily life?*
- *How do my everyday actions reflect these values?*
- *Where is there room to realign with what matters most to me?*

2. The Ripple Inventory

Try This: Draw 3 concentric circles (like ripples in water) on a page. Label them:

- Inner Ripple: *Myself and My Home*
- Middle Ripple: *My Community*
- Outer Ripple: *The Greater World*

In each circle, list 3 small ways you can create a positive impact. Then, highlight one small action from each circle you can take this week.

3. Give Yourself Grace Reflection

Journal Prompts:

- *In what ways have I shown up with intention, even when it didn't feel perfect?*
- *Where can I offer myself more grace as I juggle motherhood, career, and desire for impact?*

- *What's one kind thing I can say to myself today about the effort I'm making?*

4. Find Your Focus

Journal Prompts:

- *What issues or causes truly light me up?*
- *What strengths or resources do I already have that I can use to support that cause?*
- *What is one small, sustainable action I can take this month to contribute?*

5. Mindset Reframe Practice

Try saying or writing affirmations like:

- *Progress is better than perfection.*
- *Small actions can create big waves.*
- *I don't have to do everything; I just have to do something that matters to me.*

The ripple effect doesn't just apply to our actions. It applies to our relationship with the Earth itself.

Nature is more than something to protect. It's something that protects us. It heals us, grounds us, and reminds us what it means to be alive, connected, and part of something ancient and wise.

In the next chapter, we'll explore the sacred connection between motherhood and the natural world and how tending to the Earth becomes one of the most powerful ways we can tend to ourselves, our children, and future generations.

Because when we nurture the planet, we're not just making change—we're protecting our home.

Chapter 13

The Healing Power of Nature: Reconnecting with Ourselves through the World Around Us

Since I was a little girl, I've felt nature tug at me like the tide, constant, grounding, and full of quiet wisdom. From family cookouts in the Metroparks of Northern Ohio, to time spent at our cabin in Pennsylvania, to quiet moments at Lookout Point and feeding the birds while snow fell silently around us, nature became not just a backdrop but also a teacher.

Looking back, I'm especially grateful to my parents for giving us so much time outdoors. Whether we were hiking wooded trails, skipping stones, or simply lying in the grass and looking up at the clouds, they made nature feel like home. They didn't just encourage us to play outside; they taught us how to *be* outside, to notice, to wonder, to appreciate. Those early experiences shaped my connection to the natural world in ways I'm still discovering.

That connection deepened when I discovered the sea. I remember watching *Free Willy* and feeling something awaken inside me. I was drawn to the ocean, to the wildness beneath its surface, to the freedom and mystery it offered. I wanted to be a whale trainer and swim with dolphins, to exist in that space between reality and magic where the sea seemed to hold all the answers.

That dream evolved, but the pull of the water never left.

When I moved to Florida, I felt it again, that sense of belonging to something bigger than myself. The waves became my meditation. The salty air became my reset button. Being near the ocean reminded me that no matter how chaotic life felt, there was a rhythm, a flow, a bigger force moving beneath it all.

But it isn't just the ocean that I love. I find healing in the rustle of wind through the trees, the warmth of the sun on my face, and the stillness of forest paths. There is something deeply grounding and restorative about being surrounded by the natural world no matter the landscape.

As a certified forest therapy guide, I now have the privilege of helping others do the same. Forest therapy, rooted in the Japanese practice of *shinrin-yoku* or "forest bathing" isn't about hiking or exercise. It's about slowing down, engaging the senses, and allowing nature to bring us home to ourselves. Through my coaching work, I often integrate these gentle practices, inviting clients to take mindful walks, pause beneath trees, or simply sit in stillness and observe.

Through these shared experiences, I've witnessed something profound: When we allow ourselves to truly *be* in nature, something shifts. We soften. We remember. We reconnect not just with the world around us but with the quiet wisdom within.

And perhaps that's the greatest gift of all.

Mother Nature, to me, is not just a concept. She is a presence. A wise, generous, nurturing force that offers healing without expectation. She teaches us in seasons, not schedules. In stillness, not speed. In surrender, not struggle.

Just as we mother our children, Mother Nature mothers us all. She provides without demanding. She renews without rushing. She reminds us that everything moves in seasons, that stillness is sacred, and that growth doesn't always look linear.

When I've felt broken, overwhelmed, or lost in the noise of modern motherhood, Mother Nature has gently called me back. Sometimes through a salty breeze across my skin, sometimes through the grounding presence of dirt beneath my feet, she reminds me that I, too, am part of something wild and beautiful, that my worth is not in my productivity but in my being.

This isn't just poetic. It's deeply practical. When we immerse ourselves in nature, we lower cortisol levels, boost mood, regulate our nervous system, and reconnect with our intuitive wisdom. And when our children see us valuing this connection, they learn to do the same.

In the early, overwhelming months of raising twins, I found myself desperate for space to breathe, for a moment where I wasn't "on," where I wasn't being needed, where I wasn't juggling a million things at once. And every time I stepped outside, whether it was for a short walk, a deep breath of fresh air, or a stolen moment by the water, I felt something shift.

Nature doesn't demand anything from us. It simply exists—strong, steady, wild, free.

And in that space, I remembered something important:
We are part of this natural world. And just like the tides, just like the seasons, just like the trees that shed their leaves and bloom again, we are meant to change, to rest, to grow, to surrender to the ebb and flow of life.

As my life evolved through motherhood, my professional career, and step-parenting, so did my relationship with nature. It's no longer just a place of joy but a lifeline. When the noise of the world feels overwhelming, I return to the woods, to the water, to the wind because that's where I remember who I am.

And I know I'm not alone.

Scientific research supports what many of us feel intuitively. Studies show that time in nature improves mood and mental clarity[27] and strengthens

27 Bratman, G. N., Daily, G. C., Levy, B. J., & Gross, J. J. (2015). ***The benefits of nature experience: Improved affect and cognition***. Landscape and Urban Planning, 138, 41–50. https://doi.org/10.1016/j.landurbplan.2015.02.005

emotional regulation and resilience.[28]

There's something about being near water, breathing fresh air, standing beneath towering trees, or feeling the earth beneath our feet that reminds us of who we are at our core. It strips away the noise, the expectations, and the stress, leaving behind something pure, powerful, and deeply grounding.

I remember working in a prior PIO (Public Information Officer) role, on-call 24/7, with two phones and a full calendar. The one place I truly unplugged? The ocean. No phones. No noise. Just me and the waves. It was liberating. Today, paddleboarding, snorkeling, or simply watching the water brings me joy and gives me perspective. I hope my boys will fall in love with the water too, but more than that, I hope they find their own space in nature that gives them what the ocean gives me.

As a working mom, stepmom, and coach, I've often turned to the outdoors for moments of stillness and rejuvenation. Whether it's quietly walking through the woods, sitting by the ocean, or simply watching the sunrise, these moments remind me of the beauty and balance that exist beyond the demands of our hectic routines. Nature has an incredible ability to restore a sense of calm and perspective, offering a refreshing contrast to the noise of life. It's in these peaceful moments that I've learned to reconnect with myself, tuning into what I need, whether it's solitude, reflection, or even just the feeling of being surrounded by something bigger than myself.

Over the years, I've realized that nature has become a vital part of my self-care practice. It provides me with the space to breathe deeply, clear my mind, and reset my energy. The rhythm of the tides, the rustling of leaves, and the serenity of the natural world are all reminders that there's a flow to life that I often forget when I'm caught up in my daily to-do lists. Nature has taught me to slow down, to observe, and to listen to my body and heart. It's where I've learned to practice mindfulness, finding peace in the simple moments of life, whether it's the feeling of the sun on my skin or the sound of birds singing in the distance. These moments of connection

---

28 Kuo, M. (2015). ***How might contact with nature promote human health? Promising mechanisms and a possible central pathway***. Frontiers in Psychology, 6, 1093. https://doi.org/10.3389/fpsyg.2015.01093

with nature have been transformative, helping me cultivate a deeper sense of well-being, balance, and resilience.

As I juggle the many hats of motherhood, business, and life, nature has become my sanctuary, a space to reconnect, recharge, and reflect. It reminds me that self-care doesn't have to be complicated or time-consuming, Sometimes, all it takes is stepping outside and allowing nature's rhythms to guide me back to a place of inner peace. It's a practice I continue to cultivate, knowing that it's through these quiet moments with nature I can truly show up for myself and others—more present, more grounded, and more aligned with the life I want to live.

Nature has a way of meeting us where we are and offering gentle permission to release the pressure of perfection. The more time I've spent outdoors, the more I've learned to extend that same grace to myself. Just as the seasons shift, so do our capacities. And part of reconnecting with the Earth is also learning how to live in harmony with our reality.

That's been especially true in this chapter of life. Being a twin mom hasn't been the most sustainable season of life. I had high hopes for cloth diapers and zero-waste routines, but convenience often wins. And I've learned to make peace with that. Sustainability doesn't have to be perfect—it has to be intentional.

I do what I can: plogging, serving on the No Horsin' Around Task Force, donating to eco-causes, sharing messages of stewardship, and tuning into the broader impact of my choices. As I move beyond the baby phase and settle into our new normal, I feel ready to re-engage, not just as a mom but as a conscious citizen of the planet.

Sustainable living isn't just about green choices. It's about harmony as well. It's about showing our children how to live with intention, how to care for the Earth, and how to respect the interconnectedness of all things.

That same sense of harmony starts with how we show up in our own lives. Nature has a way of slowing us down, not just in our actions but in our awareness. It invites us to be present, to notice the moment we're in. It has taught me that awareness isn't passive; it's powerful. It means pausing long enough to feel the sun on your face before diving into your next task.

Even in my busiest seasons, I've learned that five minutes outside can shift everything. Whether it's stepping outside with my coffee, working near a window with natural light, or grounding myself barefoot in the back yard, these are the micro-moments that reconnect me to myself.

According to a study by the University of Michigan, even brief interactions with nature can enhance memory and attention span by 20%.[29] Imagine what it could do for our children and for ourselves if we wove these moments into our daily rhythm.

When we slow down enough to notice, nature has a way of reflecting the truths we often forget in our busy, modern lives.

Here are a few of the biggest lessons we can learn from the natural world:

- *The Seasons of Life*: Just like nature moves through cycles of growth, rest, and renewal, so do we. Motherhood, career, and relationships—none of these are meant to be lived at full speed all the time. It's okay to honor the season you're in.
- *The Power of Surrender*: The ocean never fights against the waves; it moves *with* them. The more we try to control every little detail of our lives, the more exhausted we become. Nature reminds us that there is power in letting go, in trusting the flow, in surrendering to what is.
- *The Importance of Stillness*: Trees don't rush their growth. The sun rises and sets every day without fail. Nature moves at its own perfect pace. When we step outside, when we pause, when we listen, we remember that we don't have to be constantly *doing* to be valuable.

---

29 Berman, M. G., Jonides, J., & Kaplan, S. (2008). The cognitive benefits of interacting with nature. *Psychological Science, 19*(12), 1207–1212. https://doi.org/10.1111/j.1467-9280.2008.02225.x

These lessons? They're all around us, whispered in the wind, woven into the tides, written in the way the Earth continues to thrive without overthinking its own existence.

But the question is: Are we paying attention?

One of the most beautiful gifts nature gives us beyond its healing and grounding power is creative clarity. As a writer, entrepreneur, and mother, I've found that my best ideas rarely come when I'm staring at a screen. They come when I'm walking beneath the trees, paddling across still water, or sitting quietly with the sun on my face.

There's something about being in nature that opens the mental floodgates. It quiets the noise of daily life and creates space for imagination to breathe. The stillness allows our subconscious to come forward. Our thoughts begin to wander, not aimlessly but productively. It's in those moments that new ideas, solutions, and inspiration surface.

In fact, research has found that exposure to natural environments enhances creative problem-solving and cognitive flexibility. A 2012 study by psychologists Ruth Ann Atchley and David Strayer showed that individuals who spent just four days immersed in nature (without access to technology) experienced a 50% increase in performance on creativity and problem-solving tasks.[30]

That creative boost doesn't require a four-day hike, though. It can be as simple as a walk around the block, journaling in a park, or even gazing out the window at a tree swaying in the breeze. Nature invites daydreaming, and daydreaming is the birthplace of creative ideas.

Whenever I feel stuck, creatively, emotionally, or mentally, I know it's time to step outside. To trade deadlines for dandelions. To exchange burnout for birdsong. Nature never fails to meet me there, ready to offer a fresh perspective and the spark of something new.

---

30 Atchley, R. A., Strayer, D. L., & Atchley, P. (2012). Creativity in the wild: Improving creative reasoning through immersion in natural settings. *PLOS ONE, 7*(12), e51474. https://doi.org/10.1371/journal.pone.0051474

Nature also doesn't have to be "out there." We can invite it in. My home is filled with houseplants, ocean-themed décor, and nature scents. These small touches ground me. They remind me of the places that make me feel most alive.

Bringing nature indoors isn't about aesthetics. It's about alignment. It's about intentionally crafting spaces that support your nervous system, your creativity, and your sense of calm. When our physical environments reflect peace, we feel more peaceful. When they reflect beauty, we feel more beautiful. And when they reflect what matters most to us—whether that's sunlight, simplicity, or a favorite seashell on the windowsill—they help us return to ourselves.

Our spaces don't have to be perfect. They just have to feel like home.

And that sense of home, the grounding, calming presence of nature, is something we can cultivate no matter where we live or how busy life gets. You don't need acres of forest or endless free time to experience the healing power of the natural world. Sometimes, the smallest shifts can create the biggest sense of connection.

Practical Ways to Infuse Nature into Your Life

Even if you're in a city, even if your schedule is full, you can still connect to the Earth:

- Start your day outside, even if it's just for 2 minutes.
- Ground yourself by walking barefoot, sitting in the grass, and breathing with intention.
- Bring nature inside with plants, essential oils, driftwood, stones.
- Unplug and take nature breaks without devices.
- Create rituals like a weekly family walk, a solo sunrise sit, or a "no-tech" picnic.

Exercises for Reflection and Connection

Exercise 1: Your Nature-Connection Ritual

- What environment do you feel most drawn to?
- What's one way you can bring more of that into your week?

Exercise 2: A Message from the Earth

- Go outside with a current challenge in mind.
- Sit, walk, or breathe for 5–10 minutes.
- What message or metaphor shows up?

Reconnecting with nature doesn't just transform us; it shapes the way we move through the world and how we raise the next generation. As we ground ourselves in the rhythms of the Earth, we naturally begin to think about what kind of world we're leaving behind for our children.

The lessons we learn from the sea, the trees, the stars, and the soil aren't just for us; they're meant to bc passed down. When we invite our children to explore the outdoors, to notice the magic in the smallest leaf or the sound of a bird's song, we're planting seeds of awareness, compassion, and responsibility.

Because just as the tides shape the shore, our values shape the hearts of our little ones.

In the next chapter, we'll explore how we can raise eco-conscious kids, not through guilt or pressure but by modeling mindfulness, curiosity, and a love for the planet they'll one day inherit.

Let's teach them to not only care for the Earth but to see themselves as part of it.

Chapter 14

Raising Eco-Conscious Kids: Teaching the Next Generation to Care for the Planet

As mothers, we're not just raising kids; we're raising future citizens of the world.

We teach them to be kind. We show them how to be brave. We guide them to be responsible. But there's another lesson that is equally essential: how to care for the Earth they'll inherit.

Because here's the truth:

- The planet we leave behind is the world they will grow up in.
- The habits we model today shape how they will treat the environment tomorrow.
- The way we speak about nature, animals, and conservation becomes the narrative they carry into adulthood.

Raising eco-conscious kids isn't about giving them a list of things they *should* or *shouldn't* do. It's about modeling a deep respect for nature, weaving environmental responsibility into their everyday lives, and empowering them to see that their actions matter.

This chapter is about small, meaningful ways to help our children love, respect, and care for the planet without it feeling overwhelming or like another item on the never-ending parenting to-do list.

Because raising eco-conscious kids? It starts with us.

One of the most important steps in raising eco-conscious kids is helping them build a genuine connection with the world around them, and that starts by gently pulling them away from screens and toward real-life experiences.

Today's children are spending more time indoors and on screens than ever before. According to the American Academy of Pediatrics, children ages 8–12 spend an average of 4–6 hours a day watching or using screens, while teens can spend up to 9 hours.[31] Meanwhile, a study from the Kaiser Family Foundation found that only 10% of children in the U.S. spend time outside daily.[32]

This shift matters, not just for their physical and emotional health but for their relationship with the planet. When children spend less time in nature, they're less likely to develop environmental awareness, empathy for living things, or a lasting appreciation for the natural world.

But the good news? This is something we can change, and it starts at home.

When we model a lifestyle that values outdoor play, exploration, and quiet observation, we help our children understand that real joy doesn't come from a glowing screen, it comes from curiosity, movement, and connection. Whether it's digging in the dirt, spotting birds, walking a nature trail, or just cloud-watching in the back yard, these experiences plant the seeds of environmental awareness and emotional resilience.

Limiting screen time isn't about restriction. It's about creating room for more meaningful connection. More laughter. More wonder. More questions about how the world works and what role we play in caring for it.

Let's give them the gift of presence. Of sunshine. Of time to wonder, explore, and belong.

---

31 American Academy of Pediatrics. (2020). ***Media and young minds***. In ***Council on Communications and Media***. Pediatrics, 138(5), e20162591. https://doi.org/10.1542/peds.2016-2591

32 Rideout, V. J., Foehr, U. G., & Roberts, D. F. (2010). ***Generation M2: Media in the lives of 8- to 18-year-olds***. Kaiser Family Foundation. https://www.kff.org/wp-content/uploads/2013/04/8010.pdf

There is something inherently magical about the way children see the world.

They are naturally curious about animals, fascinated by the ocean, eager to collect leaves, rocks, and seashells. They see the wonder in nature, something we often lose as we grow older and get caught up in the busyness of life.

And that wonder? That's the foundation for creating a generation that cares.

Research shows that children who develop a strong connection to nature are more likely to become environmentally conscious adults.[33]

Nature-connected children:

- Show higher levels of empathy for people, animals, and ecosystems.
- Develop a deeper sense of responsibility and understanding that their actions have impact.
- Grow up with a greater appreciation for the beauty of the Earth and a desire to protect it.

The more we nurture their natural connection to the world, the more they will grow up valuing and fighting for it.

Understanding why environmental education is important is only the first step. What truly makes an impact is how we bring that awareness to life in our everyday parenting. The good news? You don't need to be perfect or overhaul your entire lifestyle to raise eco-conscious kids. In fact, the most powerful lessons often come from the simple, consistent actions our children witness in their day-to-day lives.

By weaving sustainability into our routines and leading with curiosity, empathy, and intention, we can help our children grow into mindful stewards of the planet, without it feeling overwhelming for us or for them.

33 Chawla, L. (2007). Childhood experiences associated with care for the natural world: A theoretical framework for empirical results. ***Children, Youth and Environments, 17***(4), 144–170. https://www.jstor.org/stable/10.7721/chilyoutenvi.17.4.0144

Let's explore a few practical, approachable ways to make environmental responsibility a natural part of your family's rhythm.

Let Them Fall in Love with Nature

Before kids can care about protecting the Earth, they have to fall in love with it. As Jacques Cousteau famously said, *"People protect what they love."*

Try This:

- Go outdoors daily, whether it's the beach, a back yard, or a patch of grass at the park.
- Let them explore and dig in dirt, splash in puddles, collect sticks and leaves.
- Share the wonder by pointing out how clouds move, how trees sway, how birds call to one another.

When kids are immersed in nature, they develop a lasting connection to it, and that connection becomes the motivation to protect it.

However, when it comes to teaching our kids about the environment, there's a delicate line we walk as parents. We want to be honest about the challenges our planet faces, but we don't want to burden our children with fear or overwhelm. We want them to care, not carry the weight of the world on their shoulders.

So how do we teach them the truth without taking away their sense of wonder?

We lead with love. We speak with honesty. And we ground every hard truth in hope and action.

Kids are naturally empathetic, and they often feel things deeply. When we talk about pollution, endangered animals, or climate change, it's important to frame these topics not just in terms of what's wrong but also what's possible.

We can say:

- "Yes, the oceans are struggling, but look how many people are working to protect them, and here's what we can do to help."
- "Some animals are endangered, and we can be part of their story by learning about them and supporting organizations that protect them."
- "The Earth needs our care, and even small things like picking up trash or turning off lights make a difference."

This approach helps kids build what psychologists call *"eco-agency"*—the belief that they are capable of making a difference. It shifts the narrative from doom to empowerment, from helplessness to hope.

As parents, it's not our job to shield our children from the world's problems; it's to guide them with courage and compassion. We show them that while the Earth is fragile, it is also incredibly resilient. And so are they.

When we model mindful choices and honest conversations, our children learn to navigate the complexity of the world not by ignoring it but by engaging with it from a place of care, strength, and love.

When we approach these conversations with honesty, gentleness, and empowerment, we lay the groundwork for meaningful action. Our children don't need perfection; they need guidance, example, and opportunities to connect with the world around them in real, tangible ways.

And that begins at home.

Raising eco-conscious kids isn't about grand gestures. It's about weaving small, sustainable choices into everyday life, choices that teach, inspire, and nurture their natural sense of wonder and responsibility.

Let's explore some simple, meaningful ways to make environmental care a part of your family's rhythm.

Sustainability in Everyday Life

Sustainability doesn't have to be rigid—especially in motherhood and especially with twins. But every small act matters. The key is consistency and intention, not perfection.

Kids learn best when they see real-life examples, so weave environmental responsibility into your daily conversations.

Try This:

- Instead of saying *"We recycle because it's good for the planet,"* explain: *"When we recycle, this plastic bottle can be made into something new instead of ending up in the ocean."*
- At the grocery store, let them help choose fruits and vegetables without plastic packaging and explain why that matters.
- When turning off lights, say: *"We're giving our lights a rest, just like we rest our eyes when we sleep."*

By making sustainability relatable, kids start to see their actions as part of something bigger.

Lead by Example

Kids don't always do what we say but they absolutely learn from what we do.

Try This:

- Bring reusable bags to the store.
- Choose refillable water bottles instead of plastic.
- Pick up litter when you see it.
- Talk about why you make eco-friendly choices.

When kids see us caring for the Earth, it becomes second nature for them.

Reduce, Reuse, and Recycle in a Way That Makes Sense for Kids

The 3 Rs (reduce, reuse, recycle) are great concepts, but for kids, they need to be hands-on and fun.

Try This:

- Reduce: Have kids help pack lunches with reusable containers instead of plastic bags.
- Reuse: Turn old clothes into cleaning rags or cardboard boxes into art projects.
- Recycle: Set up a recycling station at home and let kids be in charge of sorting items.

Give them ownership and let it feel empowering, not burdensome.

Teach Them About the Ocean and Wildlife

As someone who feels deeply connected to the ocean, I've found it's one of the most beautiful entry points for kids to understand environmental impact.

Try This:

- Watch gentle, educational ocean documentaries together like *Blue Planet* or *My Octopus Teacher*.
- Visit aquariums or marine rescue centers to learn about ocean conservation.
- Gently explain the impact of pollution by showing how plastic affects marine life, focusing on empathy, not fear.

Making environmental issues real and tangible helps kids understand why their actions matter.

Make Giving Back a Family Tradition

Sustainability can be joyful and generous. Giving back creates a sense of purpose and shows kids that they are part of a community effort to care for the Earth.

Try This:

- Plogging: Make walks fun by picking up trash and seeing who collects the most.
- Adopt an endangered animal: For one birthday season, I gave animal adoptions as gifts. It was meaningful and memorable.
- Plant a family garden: Even a small herb pot can teach care, patience, and respect for where our food comes from.
- Shop sustainably: Show kids how "voting with your dollars" supports eco-conscious businesses.

When giving back becomes a shared family value, it teaches our children that they are part of something bigger and that their actions, no matter how small, have the power to create change.

And while these moments of community impact are powerful, it's often the everyday choices that build lasting habits. From the lunchboxes we pack to the way we shop or travel, sustainability can be woven into the fabric of daily life in ways that feel approachable, not overwhelming.

Here are some simple, practical ideas for bringing eco-conscious living into your home, your routines, and your community.

For Kids:

- Use eco-friendly diapers and wipes when possible.
- Swap toys with friends or use a toy library.
- Choose recycled and refillable school supplies.

In Daily Life:

- Pack waste-free lunches with reusable gear.
- Walk or bike for short errands.
- Carry reusable shopping bags and containers.
- Limit fast fashion and create capsule wardrobes with fewer, versatile items.

In the Community:

- Support local farmers and small businesses.
- Participate in community cleanups together.
- Write letters or create artwork to advocate for a local environmental cause.

For Wellness and Mindset:

- Prioritize experiences over things, like camping, nature walks, cloud-watching.
- Practice gratitude for the Earth through family rituals or journaling.

These small, intentional choices may seem simple, but they add up in shaping the way our families live, connect, and care for the world around us. When we normalize sustainability at home, we empower our kids to think critically, act mindfully, and take pride in being part of the solution.

To help you deepen that connection and bring these ideas to life, here are a few reflective and interactive exercises you can do together as a family because the most lasting lessons often come through shared experiences and meaningful conversations.

Exercises for Reflection and Action

Exercise 1: Create a "Nature Bucket List" with Your Kids

- Sit down with your kids and ask: *"What are 10 things you'd love to do in nature?"*
- Ideas: Go camping, see a waterfall, swim in the ocean, plant a garden, visit a wildlife sanctuary.
- Make a plan to do at least one per season!

Exercise 2: The "Eco-Hero" Challenge

- Ask your kids: "What's one way we can help the Earth this month?"
- Let them come up with an idea—it could be a litter clean-up, using less plastic, or planting a tree.
- Give them the lead in making it happen!

As parents, we won't always get it right. We'll have days when we forget the reusable bags, buy the packaged snacks, or just don't have the energy to be the perfect example.

But what matters isn't perfection. It's consistency.

When we weave small, meaningful habits into our daily lives, we plant the seeds for a generation that values the Earth.

And as our kids grow?
They won't see sustainability as an *extra task.*
They'll see it as a natural, instinctive part of life.

So, Mermaid Mama, let's raise children who don't just live in the world.
Let's raise kids who love, respect, and protect it.

When we teach our children to care for the planet, for each other, and for themselves, we're not just shaping their future. We're shaping the future of the world.

Every reusable bag packed, every nature walk taken, every small moment of mindfulness—it all matters. These daily actions might feel quiet, but they echo. They ripple.

And those ripples? They become waves.

As mothers, mentors, creators, and changemakers, we have more power than we often realize. Not because we do everything perfectly but because we lead with heart, with intention, and with the courage to try.

So as we step into the final chapter, let this be your reminder:
The way you live, love, and lead makes a mark.
You are the ripple.
You are the wave.

Let's talk about what that truly means.

Chapter 15

You Are the Ripple. You Are the Wave.

As you reach the final pages of this book, my hope for you isn't that you've found all the answers but that you've remembered you don't need to. Because the journey of motherhood, womanhood, and purposeful living was never meant to be a destination.

It's a rhythm. A rising and falling. A beautiful dance between doing and being.

You've weathered storms. You've felt the highs of joy and the lows of exhaustion. You've learned how to realign when life pulled you off course, how to create space for what matters, and how to ride the waves with grace.

But more than anything? You've awakened to your own power.

You are not just drifting in the tide of everyone else's expectations.
You are the current. The shift. The change.
You are the ripple.
You are the wave.

And every choice you make, from how you show up in your home to how you lead at work to how you nurture your body and your spirit, sends ripples outward.

Those ripples create waves. And those waves create change.

It might feel like small actions go unnoticed, but science says otherwise.

A 2023 global survey by *Edelman Trust Barometer* found that 68% of people believe that individuals, more than institutions, have the greatest power to create real change.[34]

You don't have to wait for the world to shift. You are already shifting it every time you choose presence over perfection, compassion over comparison, purpose over pressure.

If you take away anything from this book, let it be this:

You are already making a difference.

In the way you raise your children.

In the way you show up for your people.

In the way you care for the world around you.

Your story, the one you are writing every single day, is your legacy.
And it doesn't have to be grand or perfect to be meaningful.
It just has to be true.

So keep showing up. Keep choosing presence. Keep living with intention.

Because, Mermaid Mama, the world is better because you're in it.

And the waves you are creating? They will carry on farther than you can even imagine.

Let me be clear: This isn't about doing it all. You're not here to be everything to everyone.

You're here to show up authentically, intentionally, and in alignment with your values.

- You get to choose what success looks like for you.
- You get to define how your voice is used in this world.
- You get to rest. You get to grow. You get to change your mind.

---

34 Edelman. (2023). ***2023 Edelman Trust Barometer: Navigating a polarized world***. Edelman Trust Institute. https://www.edelman.com/trust/2023/trust-barometer

And most of all? You get to know that what you're doing is *enough*—even when it feels quiet, even when it feels small.

Because the quiet choices, the moments of patience, the deep breaths, the evening walks, the acts of service, those are the ripples that make up a lifetime.

You're not here to carry the weight of the world on your shoulders.

You're here to show up with heart, with purpose, and with the courage to take one meaningful step at a time. Because every small action, every intentional choice, holds the power to inspire, to uplift, and to create real change.

And when we show up together? Our ripples turn into waves.

As you reach the final pages of this book, I hope you feel a sense of clarity not because you suddenly have all the answers but because you've realized you don't need to.

Life, motherhood, career, and impact—it's not about having it all figured out. It's about learning to ride the waves, to trust the currents, to realign when needed, to pause and breathe when the waters feel overwhelming, and to dive deep when something calls to you.

You've navigated so much already. You've built a foundation that honors your identity, your family, and your work. You've learned how to let go of guilt, embrace play, create space for what matters, and realign with your purpose.

But most of all? You've recognized your own power.

If there's one thing the ocean has taught me, it's this:
We are always evolving. We are never meant to stay in one place forever.

The beauty of life isn't in arriving at some perfect destination where everything is balanced, peaceful, and figured out.

There will be days when the tide pulls back and others when it surges forward. And in all of it, you are still whole.

So as you close this book, I don't want you to walk away with a rigid plan for how to "get everything right." Instead, I hope you walk away with:

- The courage to embrace your own journey.
- The confidence to navigate the changing tides.
- The belief that your impact, big or small, matters.

And when the waves feel rough? When you doubt yourself? When you wonder if you're doing enough?

Come back to your compass. Come back to your values. Come back to the reminder that you, exactly as you are, are already creating something beautiful.

Writing this book has mirrored my own transformation, through twin motherhood, healing, and rediscovering what it means to be present and purposeful in a noisy world.

There were days I doubted whether I could finish it. Days I questioned my voice. But I came back to the waves, to the idea that even if this only reached a few hearts, that was enough.

Because impact doesn't require scale. It requires sincerity.

Thank you for letting me into your heart and home. Thank you for reading, reflecting, and riding the waves with me.

I hope these words have resonated with you, reminded you of your own power, and helped you see that you are never alone in this journey.

Let's keep riding the waves together.

If this book has inspired you, I'd love to continue the conversation! Let's stay connected:

Follow along with me on social media @laurendebick or stay up to date by visiting laurendebick.com and keep creating ripples, one choice, one action, one moment at a time.

You don't have to save the world in one day.

You just have to show up with heart, with presence, and with the belief that your life matters.

Because it does.

You are the ripple.

You are the wave.

And the world is forever changed because you were here.

With love, gratitude, and belief in your journey,

Acknowledgements

This book would not have been possible without the support, guidance, and encouragement of many individuals.

I am deeply grateful to my family for their unwavering support throughout the writing and publication of this work. To Andrew, thank you for your continued encouragement and belief in this project. To all my boys, you are a constant source of inspiration and a reminder of the importance of presence, patience, and love. Your influence is woven throughout these pages.

I owe special thanks to my own mom, whose example of strength, compassion, and resilience has shaped both my personal and professional life. Her guidance and steady support have been foundational to this work and to the values reflected within it.

I extend my sincere appreciation to my editor, Karin Nicely Lord of Seren Publishing, whose expertise, thoughtful insight, and editorial guidance were instrumental in bringing this manuscript to completion. Her ability to strengthen the work while preserving its voice was invaluable, and this book is better because of her care and commitment to the process.

I am equally grateful to my designer, Nancy R. Koucky of NRK Designs, whose creativity and attention to detail gave this book its visual identity. Her professionalism and thoughtful design work ensured that the presentation of this book aligns with its purpose and message.

I would also like to thank the friends, colleagues, and community members who offered encouragement, perspective, and support throughout this journey, often over cups of coffee, shared cheese plates, glasses of wine, and the occasional frantic afternoon phone call. These moments of conversation, reassurance, and shared experience reinforced the importance of connection and community reflected throughout this work.

Finally, I extend my gratitude to you, the reader. It is my hope that these pages offer reflection, reassurance, and encouragement, and that they serve as a meaningful companion as you navigate your own journey.

With gratitude,

About the Author

Lauren Debick is a mother of twin toddlers, stepmom to two teenage boys, certified life coach, and forest therapy guide. She is also an accomplished brand strategist with extensive experience in marketing, public relations, and community engagement, helping organizations connect meaningfully with their audiences and make a tangible impact. Lauren hosts the *Graceful Confidence* podcast, where she shares stories and insights on growth, resilience, and empowerment. She blends her professional expertise with her personal journey of motherhood and wellness to inspire women to find harmony, confidence, and purpose in every area of life. An avid runner and lover of the ocean, she draws on her own experiences navigating the tides of career, family, and personal growth to guide others toward harmony and fulfillment. *The Mermaid Mama* reflects Lauren's mission: to help women embrace their power, trust their intuition, and thrive amidst the waves of life.

www.ingramcontent.com/pod-product-compliance
Ingram Content Group UK Ltd.
Pitfield, Milton Keynes, MK11 3LW, UK
UKHW041638190726
13854UKWH00006B/2570